## DEVOTIONAL SERIES

## *LIVING ON*

### LIVING WITH

# PURPOSE Living Out

*LIVING IN*

by J. White

© 2012 by Jerry White

ISBN-978-0-9837797-1-1

All rights reserved. No part of this book may be reproduced in any form or by any electronic or mechanical means without permission in writing from the publisher, except by a reviewer who may quote brief passages or use segments of the photos in a review.

Printed in the United States of America

# Foreword

*It's important to note that this is not a 365 day devotion, daily scripture reading or daily spiritual vitamin that fluctuates with each passing day, but instead a series of devotions that will help us shed light on our season for what God intended it to be. For example, if we are dealing with a death of a loved one, we are not going to breeze through that season in twenty four hours, wake up and mask the grief with "10 steps to make a million dollars". Instead we will go through a period of grieving. In this example I'm not suggesting that we should dwell in a place of grief but I am suggesting that we should heal in our time and not be forced or distracted into the next "thing". Like obtaining wealth, grief is a process.*

*This series of devotions come under the guise of PURPOSE from knowing that oftentimes our perception about where we are or what we're going through is jaded because we aren't properly interpreting the season we're in. If I'm honest, most of us have gone with the flow of "the world" for so long that we can't even recognize spiritual situations and seasons God strategically designed or allowed to take place because we are so focused on what society says about pain, hurt, rejection, trials, uncertainties, selfishness, selflessness, patience, spontaneity, growth and most important as it pertains to "church and church folk" what it means to be blessed.*

*This is not a book of negativity or constant unpleasant circumstances but I will cover a few not so pleasant situations. Above, I chose to highlight just a few not so pleasant things we experience in life because those are the moments that have proven to be some of the most pivotal times of our journey. I purposely didn't list all the good things that come with life because none of us are in a rush to get away from those things that bring us pleasure. It's the not so good things in life that have us eager to forfeit the fire because we don't fully understand that in order to become fine china, we have to stay in the furnace long enough to fully develop and complete the process in a way that only God can perfectly hand craft. We (my mother's household) never had a china cabinet but I've been over plenty of friends' houses that do and only once can I remember somebody taking their best out of those cabinets and dining with guests. I could always tell that something extremely special needed to be taking place in order for those plates and other dining instruments to be brought down and used. I know some people that even have keys to their china cabinet as if to say something very valuable is bestowed there. It seems like who ever owned those plates wanted visitors to see it but never touch it. I'm so glad God isn't that way. Instead, God saves his best for an appointed time to put on display. But I guarantee you that God's best ALWAYS has a fire experience somewhere on their journey.*

*It has been my experience that we (Baptist, Pentecostal, Charismatic, Apostolic, and many western religions) have marketed God from a materialistic lens in an effort to portray that if God isn't blessing our money, houses, cars and careers, then God isn't blessing us. This couldn't be further from the truth.*

*This book will challenge you to not necessarily subscribe to every written word or revelation I've had but will offer different insight about very real possibilities that have been experienced not only in modern day reality but also during A.D. (After Death) and B.C. (Before Christ) time periods.*

*Whatever the case may be, I challenge you to observe your situation with spiritual eyes and ears as you read and meditate on these writings and most importantly, make the adjustments when necessary.*

# TABLE OF CONTENTS

| | |
|---|---|
| COVER | AFTER THE DRAMA |
| KNOW TO MUCH | NOT THE TIME FOR INSTINCT |
| DON'T FORGET | THANK GOD FOR BAD DEALS |
| QUIT HIDING | IMAGINE |
| GOOD NEWS, BAD NEWS, PROPHESY | |
| WHAT YOU ALLOW COULD AFFECT THOUSANDS | |
| TANGLED UP | HUMILITY |
| THE RIGHT WORDS | SIRENS |
| CHECK YOURSELF | OPEN HANDS |
| CHEERFUL GIVERS | BIT BUT NOT POISONED |
| LIKED/LOVED | YOKED |
| COMFORT | HAND |
| RECOGNIZE A TEST | PRIORITIES |
| FOLLOW DIRECTIONS | FOLLOW DIRECTIONS-PT 2 |
| LIFE | CHANGE OF HEART |
| STOP THE BLEEDING | KEEP TRUSTING |
| KEEP TRUSTING | ONE QUESTION |
| SELLOUT | PAST & VOW |
| HOW FAR | CLICHÉ' |
| RESTORED | LIFE AFTER KROGERS |
| LIFE AFTER KROGERS-PT 2 | PAY ATTENTION |
| FIGHT – PART 2 | WHAT R U WAITING FOR |
| HEART | REFLECTION |
| HARD | NEW DAY |
| PERSPECTIVE | FRONT STREET |
| ONE MAJOR GIFT | RELAX |
| WATCH THE PERKS | R U LIVING OR EXISTING |
| DON'T LOSE SIGHT | WHAT'S FOR YOU IS FOR YOU |
| WHY FAST? | ONE MORE TIME |

| | |
|---|---|
| **SHIFT** | REFLECTOR |
| **OUT OF PLACE** | HELP MIS-INTERPRETED |
| **IT DOESN'T MATTER** | STOP PURSUING |
| **FIND SOMETHING GOOD** | |
| **A CHANCE– A TOUCHABLE- THE NERVE** | |
| **DEEPER – PART 1** | DEATH |
| **DESPITE FEAR** | NEWNESS |
| **FAMILY** | HOW ARE YOU PLANTED |
| **BREAKOUT** | DIS-CONNECT |
| **WHAT ARE YOU DOING WITH IT?** | |
| **INVITATION** | useFUL or useLESS |
| **BRING'EM OUT BRING'EM OUT** | TAX TIME |
| **WHEN YOU MAKE UP YOUR MIND** | |
| **WHEN YOU MAKE UP YOUR MIND–PT 2** | |
| **SURVIVE** | YOU START IT |
| **WEARY** | THE BANK |
| **IT TAKES NERVE** | U O BAY |
| **TURN OF EVENTS** | FINDING YOUR PURPOSE |
| **WHAT WOULD THEY SAY** | RESOLUTIONS |
| **STILL SOME FIGHT LEFT IN YOUR** | |
| **INTIMIDATED** | |
| **WHEN YOU KNOW THAT YOU KNOW** | |
| **WORTHLESS** | AMBITION VS ABILITY |
| **SUDDENLY** | SUDDENLY – PART 2 – REVIVAL |
| **IS YOUR LEADER HELPING YOU?** | LOST |
| **THE PATH** | EVER BEEN HUMILIATED |
| **THE SPOT** | KEEP LISTENING |
| **WALKING INTO AN OPPORTUNITY** | |
| **NECESSARY BETRAYAL** | PENALTY |
| **HEARTS** | SADNESS – PART 1 |
| **SADNESS–PART 2: THE REQUEST** | |
| **DETERMINATION: ENDING THE SADNESS** | |

| | |
|---|---|
| **CLEAR IT OUT** | **READY** |
| **GO BACK** | **PUSHED OUT** |
| **PUSHED OUT–PART 2** | **RE-ROUTED** |
| **IN THE FURNACE** | **WE MUST TURN** |
| **NURTURED DIVIDENDS** | **WENT TO FAR** |
| **HELP ME OVERCOME MY UNBELIEF** | |
| **SIN WITHIN** | **THE FLESH** |
| **EVER FELT LIKE A FOOL?** | **PLAY YOUR ROLE** |
| **GOD STARTED IT** | |
| **WHOSE YEAST DO U PARTAKE** | |
| **DOUBLE FOR YOUR TROUBLE** | **CROSS IT – BUT** |
| **SIMPLE TRUTH** | **IF IT WAS ME** |
| **TRUTH TESTED** | **WHAT CHAPTER ARE YOU IN** |
| **MIGHT AS WELL** | **IS IT WORTH IT** |
| **EVER WONDERED?** | **GOD KNOWS YOU'RE SCARED** |
| **THE DASH** | **PLANTED FOR A PURPOSE** |
| **MIS-INTERPRETED SACRIFICE** | |
| **WHEN THE FORCE IS AGAINST YOU** | |
| **BLOCKED FOR YOUR PROTECTION** | |
| **EVICTED** | |

**COVER**

20th chapter of (First) 1 Samuel.

SUMMARY-Saul was plotting to kill David but God had already revealed. This fact to David. As a result, David asked Jonathan (Saul's son) if he could go away because he knew that Saul intended to kill him. Jonathan was in denial at first but soon came to realize that David's intuition was correct. David could no longer stay but instead had to flee for his life.

-This is the type of situation where you find out what it means to be a real FRIEND.

--It is important to note that Jonathan is the son of the King, and next in line to take over the throne.

-This next response from Saul came as a result of Jonathan allowing David to go away to his family. (verse 30) Saul's anger flared up at Jonathan and he said to him, "You son of a perverse and rebellious woman! Don't I know that you have sided with the son of Jesse to your own shame and to the shame of the mother who bore you? As long as the son of Jesse lives on this earth, neither you nor your kingdom will be established. Now send and bring him to me, for HE MUST DIE!" -Jonathan was next in line for the throne and all he had to do was mislead David and bring him back to the King, but instead, he sent David away.

*REVELATION/UNDERSTANDING*-Jonathan had everything to gain by having David killed but his Love and Loyalty toward God and David, wouldn't allow him to give David up for death.

QUESTION: Have you ever had the opportunity to get someone in trouble for a mistake they made but didn't? Have you ever been the one who made the mistake but you had a friend who covered you rather than exposed you?

-FRIENDS COVER YOU! BUT FRIENDS ALSO CORRECT YOU. FRIENDS WANT TO SEE YOU PROSPER, EVEN WHEN IT MEANS THEM MISSING OUT OR PUTTING THEMSELVES ON THE BACK BURNER.

-Friends are TRULY happy for you when you get married even though they are still single; Friends won't sleep with your man/woman even if the opportunity presents itself; Friends will sacrifice for you to keep your family together; and Friends won't allow a position to come between you and them as was the case with David and Jonathan.

-Friends won't hold what they did for you over your head either.

What type of FRIEND are YOU?

## AFTER THE DRAMA

I Samuel chapter 19 brought a few things to mind.

-Saul wanted to kill David because he killed Goliath – TRUTH!

-What's fascinating is the fact that everybody else, including Saul, had the same opportunity to stand up and face the giant that David did. David was the only one courageous enough to step out and do what they considered to be, THE IMPOSSIBLE.

REVELATION/UNDERSTANDING: Isn't it strange how people you grew up with have/had the same opportunities to get an education as you did, but they didn't do the work? Now they are mad at you because you've moved on! They say things like, "you think your special!" NO, "I KNOW I'M SPECIAL!"

-Part of the hate that Saul harbored was because he was "the king" yet along came some boy who did what he was afraid to do.

-Don't apologize for flexing in your anointing. (verse 4) Jonathan spoke well of David to Saul his father and said to him, "Let not the king do wrong to his servant David; he has not wronged you, and what he has done has benefited you greatly. (verse 5) He took his life in his own hands when he killed the Philistine. The Lord won a great victory for all Israel, and you saw it and were glad.

--Funny how people try to get rid of you after all the dirty work is done! People will release you after the hardest work is completed and you're over the hump. Now they don't need you anymore.

***Notice how God used the people closest to Saul to fight for David, His son Jonathan and his daughter Michal.

CONCLUSION: God has strategically placed people in position to bless you. Your job is to remain faithful and obedient to Him. The people who you don't expect to help you will be the very ones to cover you. Maybe you're that covering for someone else.

**KNOW TO MUCH**

Let's look at I Samuel chapter 17. This is the story about David and Goliath. Many of us might've heard this story, but there are a few details that are significant that we may overlook. (verse 32) David said to Saul (the King), "Let no one lose heart on account of this Philistine; your servant will go and fight him." (verse 33) Saul replied, "You are not able to go out against this Philistine and fight him; you are only a boy, and he has been a fighting man from his youth."

*REVELATION/UNDERSTANDING-* People are quick to discount your ability because they are focused on the wrong thing. People tend to want to quote FACTS and STATS, but will ignore the TRUTH.

-The TRUTH is that David had something at that time that everybody else in the camp lacked and that was FAITH &

WORKS. IMPORTANT NOTE: One is not good without the other. You can't have faith and no works and you can't work without faith (when you are doing kingdom things [Whosoever hath ears let them hear]). We often have the FAITH but won't do the WORK! Some of us don't know how to do anything except work (and work hard) but we are working toward something we can SEE or achieve on OUR OWN ability.

FAITH & WORKS- James 2: 26 "As the body without the spirit is dead, so FAITH without WORKS is dead. "WHY DID DAVID HAVE THE FAITH HE HAD? verse 34-But David said to Saul, "Your servant has been keeping his father's sheep. When a lion or a bear came and carried off a sheep from the flock, I went after it, struck it and killed it. Your servant hath killed both the lion and the bear; this uncircumcised Philistine will be like one of them, because he has defied the armies of the living God. The Lord who delivered me from the PAW of the lion and the PAW of the bear will deliver me from the HAND of this Philistine."

\*\*God has given us previous victories in our lives that should've built our faith. Some of us have been given great assignments in our lives and God has already showed us that with HIM, we can do all things.

--Without you, the company wouldn't be what it is, so why are you afraid to start your own, (especially when you think about it all the time)?

--You were sent there to learn, not to get comfortable and COMPLAIN-cent!!

--David not only fought for some people who were afraid, but he also fought for a cause.

--YOU GOTTA DO WHAT GOD IS CALLING YOU TO DO BECAUSE PEOPLE ARE DEPENDING ON YOU! NOT JUST BECAUSE YOU WILL SAVE THEM, BUT also BECAUSE THE ACTIONS YOU TAKE ON FAITH WILL ENCOURAGE THEM TO TAKE THEIR OWN STEP OF FAITH.

I can be here all day on this so I'll close with these two commands; 1. QUIT EXISTING AND START LIVING 2. DO THE WORK!


**NOT THE TIME FOR INSTINCT**
I Samuel chapter 13.
SUMMARY-Saul is the King over Israel at this particular time and HIS SON (Jonathan) started a battle with the Philistines (verse 3).
-Here comes dad (King Saul) to the rescue.
The problem is, Saul and his men were greatly outnumbered which resulted in him and his men running and hiding (verse 6-7).
IMPORTANT TO NOTE: (verse 7) Saul remained at Gilgal, and all the troops with him were quaking with fear. (verse 8) He waited seven days, the TIME SET BY SAMUEL (referring to chapter 10 verse 8); BUT SAMUEL DID NOT COME TO GILGAL, and Saul's men began to scatter. (verse 9) So he said," Bring me the burnt offering and the fellowship offering." And Saul offered up the burnt offering. Just as he finished making the offering, Samuel arrived, and Saul went out to greet him. (verse 11) "What have you done?" asked Samuel. Saul replied, "When I saw that the men were scattering, and that you did not come at the set time, and that the Philistines were assembling at Micmash, I THOUGHT, 'Now the Philistines will come down against me at Gilgal, and I have NOT SOUGHT THE LORD'S FAVOR.' so I FELT compelled to offer the burnt offering."
REVELATION/UNDERSTANDING: There have been times and there will be times in our lives when we have to make split second decisions. THIS IS NOT ONE OF THEM! DO NOT MOVE YET! If God has given you SPECIFIC instructions, you wait on Him. It doesn't matter how astray or helter-skelter

things may be in your life right now, WAIT! YES, the money may be getting a little tight! YES, you want to marry this particular individual! YES, doors have closed all around you! YES, you are in the midst of a heated battle, be it work, home or school!

DON'T TAKE MATTERS INTO YOUR OWN HANDS!

-Things may LOOK one way to your naked eyes, but God has a set of lenses that sees something totally different.

THIS IS NOT THE TIME FOR INSTINCT, THIS IS THE TIME FOR PRAYER, AND MAYBE EVEN FASTING.

CONCLUSION- (verse 13) "You acted foolishly," Samuel said. "You have not kept the command the Lord your God gave you; IF YOU HAD, He would have established your kingdom over Israel for all time. But now your kingdom will not endure; the Lord has sought out a man after His own heart and appointed him leader of his people, because you have not kept the Lord's command." -NOW IS NOT THE TIME TO BE FOOLISH, NOW IS THE TIME TO GET EVEN CLOSER TO GOD.

## DON'T FORGET

I Samuel chapter 12. The word for this season is "Don't Forget" Samuel spends this entire chapter giving the Children of Israel a history lesson on how it was their God who fought all of their battles for them and brought them out of bondage starting from Moses and Aaron up to now.

---*REVELATION/UNDERSTANDING*—We have a responsibility to each generation to tell them about God and the things He has done for us.

-Our biggest problem is the FACT that we often FORGET what God has done for us.

--QUIET TIME--Take some time TODAY to remember what God has done for you and for us as a people.

CONCLUSION: This past Saturday, myself and two others went to eat at a restaurant on 14th street here in Atlanta. The place reminded me of an old segregated diner where blacks could not enter, let alone enter through the front door.

-Individually, God has brought me through some tough times and miraculous endeavors.

COLLECTIVELY- Fifty short years ago, blacks couldn't ride on the front of a bus or drink water from a white's only fountain. Fifty short years ago, blacks couldn't vote. A few years earlier than that, blacks couldn't even get an education. Some people even considered blacks less than a human being. Look how far God has brought us.

-We have more CEO's now than ever. We have more business owners now than ever. We have more politicians now than ever. We have more spokesman now than ever. We have more actors/directors now than ever.

-BUT WE STILL AREN'T THERE YET.

-We've forgotten! We've forgotten! We've forgotten!

Take some time today to remember what God has done for you, me and us. As great as Dr. King was, it was not about him. It was and still is, all about God.

Praise Him!

## THANK GOD FOR BAD DEALS

I Samuel chapter 11. verse 1-2, Nahash the Ammonite went up and Besieged Jabesh Gilead (Children of Israel). And all the men of Jabesh said to him, "Make a treaty with us, and we will be subject to you." (verse 2) But Nahash (the enemy) the Amorite replied," I will make a treaty with you ONLY on the condition that I gouge out the right eye of every one of you and so bring disgrace on all Israel."

*REVELATION/UNDERSTANDING:* I don't know about you but that sounds like a bad deal.

-You and me would be slaves for somebody right now if it wasn't for a bad deal. For some of us it's a contract, for some of us its a salary, for some of us its an automobile or house, for some of us it's a relationship. I don't know who this is for, but You don't have to settle for being the OTHER woman! It may hurt JUST FOR A MINUTE to be by your self, but being the OTHER woman is a bad deal!!

If Nahash would've been content with the Children of Israel just serving him, the turnout would've been different but as a result of his bad offer, it resulted in catastrophe for him and his people. The enemy will ALWAYS make a mistake. The problem is however; that we are not paying attention to God (the teacher) but instead we focus on the enemy (the student). It was the enemy who had Paul and Silas brutally beaten for casting a spirit out of a young woman. The mistake the enemy made however; was not stopping with the beating. They had Paul and Silas thrown in Jail TOGETHER where they sang praises to the Lord to the point where the whole prison shook and the gates swung open.

END RESULT- The jail keeper and his whole family became believers and got saved. Thank God for the enemy always going overboard PUT YOUR FOOT DOWN-There comes a point in everyone's life when we are going to have to put our foot down and demand respect. That moment came for Saul.

(verse 6) When Saul heard their words, the Spirit of God came upon him in power, and he burned with anger.

ANGER- is good when it is used to fight against injustice or Un-godliness.

QUESTION-Why does it take an event to upset our conditions before we decide that change is necessary?

verse 7-Saul took a pair of oxen, cut them into pieces, and sent the pieces by messengers throughout all Israel, proclaiming, "This is what will be done to the oxen of anyone who does not follow Saul and Samuel."

--LEADERSHIP- (I know who this is for)- Learn how to galvanize an mobilize your people.

## QUIT HIDING

1 Samuel chapter 10. In this chapter, Saul was anointed King over Israel and a few things took place during the process. verse 17, Samuel summoned the people of Israel to the Lord at Mizpah and said to them, "This is what the Lord, the God of Israel, says: 'I brought Israel up out of Egypt, and I delivered you from the power of Egypt and all the kingdoms that oppressed you.' (19) But you have now rejected your God, who saves you out of all your calamities and distresses. And you have said, 'No, set a king over us.' So now present yourselves before the Lord by your tribes and clans."

QUESTION: Have you pushed the leadership of God in your life aside, in an effort to follow someone or something? Who has become your king or ruler?

-Yes! We may have bosses or supervisors. We may even have pastors and ministers, but none of those things should override your relationship with God. When you spend time with God, especially in prayer, He will give you the answers you need. Your boss, or pastor will confirm what God says and it will line up. OR, God will speak to you and show you an upcoming situation so that you won't get bent out of shape trying to follow what YOU consider to be the end all, be all.

verse 21- Finally Saul, the son of Kish was chosen. But when they looked for him, he was not to be found. So they inquired further of the Lord, " Has the man come here yet?" And the Lord said, "Yes, he has hidden himself among the baggage."

*REVELATION/UNDERSTANDING*-Quit running or hiding from what God has anointed you to do. Don't let the FEAR of FAILURE or INADEQUACY stop you from stepping into your role, position, and duty.

-God will make provision for you!

RIDICULOUS-Saul stood a foot taller than everybody else and had the nerve to try to hide (verse 23). You are a giant to some people whether it be a PRAYER giant, WARRIOR spirit, giant of FAITH, GIVER, or LEADER. Do it and do it like the giant you are. QUIT HIDING behind who GOD made you to be!!! LOVED and HATED- (verse 26) Saul also went home in Gibeah, accompanied by valiant men whose hearts God had touched. (27) But some troublemakers said, "How can this fellow save us?"

-You CANNOT please everybody. You will be loved and hated at the same time. The sooner you accept that, the better off and better equipped you will be to handle your anointing. YOU ARE GOING TO BE LOVED AND HATED! The sooner you ACCEPT that, the better off and better equipped you will be to handle YOUR ANNOINTING!

**IMAGINE**
I Samuel chapter 7. After I finished studying, I spent time meditating and I came up with this question. CAN YOU IMAGINE HOW GOD WOULD FEEL IF WE AAALLLLL SERVED HIM ON ONE ACCORD? (verse 3) Samuel said to the WHOLE house of Israel," If you are returning to the Lord with all your hearts, then rid yourselves of the foreign gods and the Ashteroths and commit yourselves to the Lord and
serve Him only, and He will deliver you out of the hand of the Philistines."
COMMENTARY
-The idols that we have today are a bit more subtle than their gods of wood and stone but they are just as dangerous. Whatever holds first place in our lives or controls us is our god. Be it money, success, material goods, pride or people. We must let nothing rival Him (author unknown).

"IF" in verse three suggests condition or conditional circumstances. If you do this, "then" I will do that. But not until the if is carried out. We often want something for nothing but it doesn't work like that. If you study and apply yourself, you'll do well in school. If you pay your tithes, then all of your needs will be met. If you sow good seeds, you'll reap good harvest.

If you sow bad seeds, you'll get bad harvest. If you put away your idols, then God will work on your behalf. If you DON'T put away your idols, then you'll be left to fight on your own. I don't know about you, but I need God to fight on my behalf.

## GOOD NEWS, BAD NEWS, PROPHECY

I Samuel chapter 6. Summary- The ark of the Lord was in the Philistines camp for seven months and because of that, God brought plagues of tumors upon them. The Philistines finally decided that they needed to get rid of the ark so they sent it away on a cart that was pulled by two cows. Not only did they send the ark away, but they also sent with it a GUILT offering. The Philistines didn't know where the cows would take it, so they followed the cart (which went to Beth Shemesh v.12). This brings us to the word for the day.

verse 13- Now the people of Beth Shemesh were HARVESTING their wheat in the valley, and when they looked up and saw the ark, they rejoiced at the sight. GOOD NEWS- Some of us have been in a season where we haven't felt the presence of God as strong as we used to. It was a test to see if we would still walk with Him. We struggled with our prayer life, we struggled with our hearing, we struggled with our fasting, we struggled with our mission/purpose, we struggled with giving, some of us even backslid. But God IS restoring His closeness and presence. Not because we deserve it! Not because we sent for Him! Not because we were the most faithful! God is restoring Himself to those who yearn for Him because we NEED Him.

--NOTICE- The people of Beth Shemesh were in a season of harvest when the ark of the Lord returned. -In spite of God distancing Himself from us for a season, some of us still prospered. Some of us made more money, acquired more things, made new friends, took more trips and gained higher positions.

-OFFERING-What are YOU (and I stress YOU) willing to sacrifice to God for returning closer to YOU?

verse 15- "On that day the people of Beth Shemesh offered burnt offerings and made sacrifices to the Lord."

(verse 19) But God struck down some of the men of Beth Shemesh, putting seventy of them to death because they had LOOKED into the ark of the Lord. The people mourned because of the heavy blow the Lord had dealt them, and the men of Beth Shemesh asked, "Who can stand in the presence of the Lord, this holy God?"

BAD NEWS- There WILL be some casualties in your life. (That doesn't necessarily mean that some people will literally die). It means that God's presence in your life will make some people leave you or make you leave some people. It means that you might possibly have to leave your job or you may get fired.

--NOT EVERYONE CAN BE IN THE PRESENCE OF GOD

-Some people will LOOK to closely at you as you walk with God and as He walks with you and will fall away (or become casualties in your life because they can't stand His presence.

OBVIOUSLY- There will be some mourning but let them go! Let him go! Let her go! Let it go!

PRAISE HIM

## WHAT YOU ALLOW COULD AFFECT THOUSANDS

I Samuel Chapter 4.

(verse2) The Philistines deployed their forces to meet Israel, and as the battle spread, Israel was defeated by the

Philistines, who killed about four thousand of them on the battlefield. (verse 3) When the soldiers returned to the camp, the elders of Israel asked, "Why did the Lord bring defeat upon us today before the Philistines?" In this chapter, God literally keeps His word about destroying the house of Eli (the priest) because Eli did not restrain his sons from sinning (Chapter 3:13-14). The prophecy came from Chapter 2 verse 27-36 (please read).

WHY? WHY? WHY? (chapter 2 verse 29) " Why do you honor your sons more than me by fattening yourselves on the choice parts of every offering made by my people Israel?"

*-REVELATION/UNDERSTANDING-* LEADERSHIP-Be careful what you do with God's money!

--"Why do you honor your sons more than me?"

--Some of us allow our children to do anything they want to do rather than doing what is honorable to God.

--Some of us witness behavior that is ungodly and we allow it to continue because we're afraid that somebody won't like us.

If somebody is stealing and you know about it, you better say or do something about it! If somebody you know is doing anything contrary to what is ethical in God's eyes, you better say something. It's one thing to not know, but you are just as accountable if you know and continue to let it go on.

After you give the warning, the rest is up to them. BUT YOU MUST DO YOUR PART --WHENEVER WE PUT PEOPLE/THINGS BEFORE GOD'S HAPPINESS, THERE WILL BE CONSEQUENCES.

As a result of Eli allowing the behavior by his sons to persist 34,000 people were killed! (verse10)

NOT THE MOST ENTHUSIASTIC DEVOTION, BUT IT IS WHAT IT IS. I GUESS IT DEPENDS ON HOW YOU LOOK AT IT.

## TANGLED UP

Psalm 31. There are 9 verses but let's focus on the middle two

(4 & 5). "Free me from the trap that is set for me, for you are my refuge. (verse 5) Into your hands I commit my spirit; redeem me, O Lord, the God of truth."

--In verse 4, the writer uses the word "trap" and is using it in the future tense. He is not yet caught in the trap, but understands that a trap has been set and therefore is asking God to FREE him even though he hasn't been tangled up or caught in the trap.

--He had enough wisdom to know that a trap has been set for him, and even more wisdom to ask God to free him before he even gets tangled up. REMEMBER, A TRAP IS NOT DESIGNED TO LOOK LIKE A TRAP.

-When you are in relationship with God, the enemy (Satan) is doing everything Satan can to get you caught up in a trap. It could be a bad relationship, a money scheme, a sexual situation, or even deter you away from your purpose (which might be the worst of them all).

QUESTION: Have you ever seen a trap, been outside of a trap, not yet caught in the trap, but are already trying to figure out a way out of the trap?

-DON'T GET TANGLED UP IN THE TRAP!!!!!! YOU SEE IT COMING, GO THE OTHER WAY!!!!!!!!!

-The writer PRAYED to GOD to free him before he gets caught up. (I can quit right here, and go eat some barbecue).

-VERSE 5- "I commit my spirit into your hands."

-That's the way we make it ladies and gentlemen, by committing our spirits into God's hands.

--PRAYER--Lord, thank you for not allowing the enemy to trip me up. Thank you for detonating the trap before I got to it.

Please receive my spirit into your hands and guide me. In Christ name I pray, and ask it all. AMEN

## HUMILITY

Matthew chapter 3.

This is the part of John's ministry where he baptizes Jesus. (verse 13) Then Jesus came from Galilee to the Jordan to be baptized by John. (14) But John tried to deter him saying, "I need to be baptized by you, and do you come to me?" (15) Jesus replied, "Let it be so now; it is proper for us to do this to fulfill all righteousness." Then John consented.

*REVELATION/UNDERSTANDING*: There is a time to be obedient and a time to be humble.

-Jesus had to be humble enough to be baptized by a sinner and John had to be humble enough to do it (not high minded).

-Be humble enough to receive. Don't be so prideful.

-Sometimes people will try to do things for you but you won't let them because YOU perceive that they can't afford to give it or you have more than them.

***I must say, that you still have to discern the motive*****

-John felt unworthy to baptize Jesus.

QUESTION-Have you ever felt unworthy to receive something/someone? It seems like we aught to give God some thanks when this happens. Be grateful and move on.

## THE RIGHT WORDS

John Chapter 5 informs us of a man that had been lame/paralyzed for 38 long years. Jesus shows up and here is their dialogue. (verse 6) "When Jesus saw him lying there and learned that he had been in this condition for a long time he asked him, 'Do you want to get well?' (verse 7) 'Sir', the invalid replied, 'I have no one to help me into the pool when the water is stirred. While I am trying to get in, someone else goes down ahead of me.' (verse 8) Then Jesus said to him, 'get up! Pick up your mat and walk.'"

*REVELATION/UNDERSTANDING*-Jesus OBSERVED that the man had been in that condition for a long time. In other words, Jesus paid attention. The place was crowded but Jesus paid attention to him.

-- (verse 7) People are out for themselves. You think people want you to get healed/blessed before they do?

-- Then Jesus asked him one simple question. "Do you want to get well?" By his response, it tells us that he was trying to set it up with Jesus to put him in the water but Jesus wasn't there for that. The man was desperate but who can blame him? He'd been in that condition for 38 years.

-Jesus didn't ask him anything about the water. He asked him a yes or no question.

-Although Jesus' question seemed to be ridiculous, some people don't want their conditions to change, they are cool with poverty. They are cool with no education. They are cool with generational curses. Especially when they've been that way for so long. Not just them, but their parents and grandparents. RIGHT WORDS- There are people that we know who have been in an unfavorable state for a long time, but if we'd take a moment to pay attention to them, we can heal them. A word from YOU, A WINNER, AN ACHIEVER, AN ACCOMPLISHER, A GOAL SETTER, A PIONEER, A PRAYER WARRIOR, A BEACON OF LIGHT, A LEADER, could change a persons' life forever. Most of the time, people are focused on the wrong things.

****What works for everybody else is not supposed to work for you*****

-JESUS-said the right words to him. "Take up your mat and walk"

-COMMAND- It was a command! He didn't ask him if he would like to pick up his mat and walk, he commanded him to. You don't wait for someone else to help you do it, YOU do it! When you do decide to do it, God will send the people to help you.

PARTICIPATION- Jesus didn't take up his bed for him, nor did He put him in the water. The man had to participate in his healing. You've got to do your part. You've got to participate.

--ASSIGNMENT--Go to someone who has been in a negative state for a while and speak the words "GET UP! AND BE WHAT GOD COMMISSIONED YOU TO BE" As soon as they try to make an excuse or explain like the man did, just keep saying GET UP! Have a wonderful and inspiring day and remember that, a WORD from YOU will change somebody's life forever!

## SIRENS

As I write to you, I literally hear sirens. Sirens represent help is on the way. Sirens also alert people to get out of the way because there is someone in greater need than you/me getting to work, going shopping, or getting to our destination. In order for help to be on the way, there has to be somebody in need of that help. Imagine how the person or people in need must feel when they hear the sound of the sirens getting closer and closer. What a relief it must be to know that, even though there is pain, help is getting closer and closer.

-WISDOM- The sirens are sounding all over the world but the good news is that Help is on the way. Are you relieved or are the sirens mute in your life? Are you to focused on yourself and getting to your destination to the point where you don't hear the sirens, therefore you won't pull over?

**CHECK YOURSELF**

1 John chapter 3. In this chapter, the writer is referencing love. Before I reference the scripture, I just want you to take a minute to think about that word LOVE. Then I want you to take a minute and think about this statement "Am I truly an example of Jesus in the form of LOVE?" Look at what He says in verses 20, "if a man say, I love God, and hates his brother, he is a liar: for he that loves not his brother whom he hath seen, how can he love God whom he hath NOT seen?"

REVELATION/UNDERSTANDING- Most of us claim to love kinsman, friends, and humankind as a whole, but do we really *know* what love is? Sometimes we will act as if we love a person/people until they do something to offend us, then we flip the script on them. Did we ever really love that person/people? The moment someone takes something away from us, or repossesses something, we quickly stop loving them. Did we ever love them at all? Those are a few examples of how we sometimes act. In this particular text, the writer is talking about something different. He is asking us to check ourselves. Pay attention to his question. How do you treat people? (Irregardless of how they treat you) Depending on your job/schedule, you and I will see a number of humankind today (not just strangers), but are so caught up in self that we don't realize that the love we "say" we are or possess, is needed by an individual(s). Somebody needs your touch today. Somebody needs your smile today. Somebody needs your ear today. And yes, somebody needs some of your money today.

SOLUTION- Let's try to BE love.

PLEASE read 1 Corinthians chapter 13 verses 1-13.

I don't know who you are, but you have a home that is VACANT. You are to put someone that is without a home, in your home. The person/people who you are to put in your home will be revealed to you. Don't FOCUS on how the bills will get paid. BE OBEDIENT!

## OPEN HANDS

In 2 Corinthians Chapter 9, Paul is writing to the Corinthians reminding them about their pledge to give a certain amount to the needy. Even though they were eager to give (verse 2), Paul still wanted to send some of his disciples to make sure that they (the Corinthians) were READY to give so that when the time came, it wouldn't catch them off guard and the giving that was meant to be done cheerfully, wouldn't turn to grudgingly.

PREPARE:

-You can be eager to give, but unprepared to give. When you are unprepared to give, it disappoints the people who were depending on you, therefore will cause God to lack some praise that He would've gotten. Ministry is all about giving.

God gave His only begotten son (John 3:16), Jesus gave His life for us and the ministry. (Matthew, Mark, Luke, John)

-What greater gift is there than being able to give someone something that they NEED when they are cognizant of the fact that they need it? How much more appreciation will they have when they KNOW that they don't deserve it?

QUESTION- Have you ever received something that you needed right when you needed it most? Even in spite of your sinful ways? When this occurs, a few things happen.

1. It makes a person appreciative (some more than others)
2. It builds faith to the point that if the need was supplied then, it will be supplied again.
3. It (in many cases) is the bridge that builds a relationship with the person or people.
4. It makes them think about giving when they see someone else in need.

5. (For most believers) the person or people praise God for supplying their needs. (Who may not have come down Himself and placed it in your lap, but He put it on someone's heart to come and give to you.

-Paul bragged about them being ready to give (verse 3). Notice also how he stresses how to give out of what is in your heart as opposed to out of compulsion (verse 7) "Each man should give what he has decided in his heart to give, not reluctantly or under compulsion, for God loves a cheerful giver. (verse 8) And God is able to make all grace abound to you, so that in all things at all times, having all that you need, you will abound in every good work." Now He who supplies seed to the sower and bread for food will also supply and increase your store of seed and will enlarge the harvest of your righteousness.

-It is God's job to supply your needs (when you are obedient to Him). As we give, He replenishes so that we can continue to give.

-MANY OF US DON'T HAVE BECAUSE WE DON'T HAVE THE HEART TO GIVE. WE ARE SELFISH AND ARE SEEKING THINGS FOR VANITY OR TO BE SEEN. We want the cars, jewels and clothes so we can floss and show off, having forgotten who it was that gave us the stuff (or the power to get the stuff) in the first place, as opposed to using the stuff to witness of how good God has been. Then we say that it all belongs to God but get an attitude when He puts it on our hearts to give it away. We (especially Americans) tend to think that the more you have is symbolic of being Godly or "blessed". Please take a few moments to read 1 Timothy 6: 3-6 I have so much more to share but have to go now, please meditate on this word and we'll talk later.  Closer than you think!

**CHEERFUL GIVERS**

2 Corinthians chapter 8. Look at what Paul writes to the Corinthians about giving in verses 10-12," And here is my advice about what is best for you in this manner: Last year you were the first not only to give but also to have the desire to do so. Now finish the work, so that your eager willingness to do it may be matched by your completion of it, according to what one has, not according to your means. FOR IF THE WILLINGNESS IS THERE, THE GIFT IS ACCEPTABLE ACCORDING TO WHAT ONE HAS, NOT ACCORDING TO WHAT HE DOES NOT HAVE."

*REVELATION/UNDERSTANDING:* Many times we focus on what the preacher is driving or wearing instead of *our* relationship with God. If they want to do the wrong things with the money then that's THEIR problem. You do your part and give with a cheerful heart. We don't know why God places the people He does in position and we really aught not question Him. Our job is to give cheerfully out of what *He* has given US. Some of us have been scarred because while we have been struggling, the preacher is living fat (Understandable) therefore we don't want to give to the church as we should. This is why God says give CHEERFULLY out of what you have, not out of what you don't have. Don't give your pamper or rent money because there's a good chance that you'll be bitter when its rent time or your baby needs pampers and you don't have it to pay for. Giving is a spiritual principle that allows us to honor God with some of what He has given us. (Deuteronomy 8:18 says, God gives us the power to get wealth).

-Anything given grudgingly isn't really giving

Read Mark 12:41-44. This is the story about the widow who truly gave.

CLOSING REMARKS: There are some of us who WOULD give IF we could, and there are some of us who CAN give but WON'T. Which are you?

## BIT BUT NOT POISONED

Acts Chapter 28, Paul and 276 passengers were on their way to Rome by boat when they suddenly were halted by a horrific storm. The storm was so intense that it tore the boat into pieces and cast them upon an island. The conditions were horrible, being cold and rainy. It was to the point where they had to kindle a fire to keep warm. (verse 3) "And when Paul had gathered a bundle of sticks, and laid them on the fire, there came a viper (venomous snake) out of the heat, and fastened on his hand. (verse 4) And when the barbarians saw the venomous beast hang on his hand, they said among themselves, No doubt this man is a murderer, whom, though he hath escaped the sea, yet vengeance suffers not to live."

*REVELATION/UNDERSTANDING*- Even when you are trying to be of service, someone will try to infect you with their poison. It could be lying, backbiting, gossiping, stealing, adultery, getting high, etc. Some people are just NEGATIVE. Their only purpose for coming to work is to see whose day they can ruin. Some people come to the party just to start a fight. Some people invite you out with the "clique" just to make you the butt of their jokes to lift themselves up to be more than they really are.

JUDGES- Look at verse four. Some people automatically judge you by what God allows to happen to you. You may be going through a storm commissioned by God but onlookers have already judged you by their own standards.

PAY ATTENTION: God allows the storms for a few reasons. To blow some things/people out of your life, to bring in some new things/people into your life, to show YOU who really has your back. Sometimes you'll have to ask some people who were close to you "When did you switch?"

RESULT- (verse 5) "And he (Paul) shook off the beast into the fire, and felt NO harm." You've got to shake some things off of you. You've got to rid yourself of negative people. You can't let everything affect you. Yes, they meant for it to poison you. Yes they even meant for it to take you out, but it only has life if YOU allow it to stay attached to you. Shake it off! Shake him off! Shake her off! Shake them off!

CHILD OF GOD- (verse 6) "Howbeit, they looked when he should have swollen, or fallen down dead suddenly: but after they had looked a great while, and saw no harm come to him, they changed their minds, and said that he was a god."

--When you are being attacked, and people are passing judgment, and people are turning their backs on you, and people leave your side and take the other side, and when people THINK you are getting what you deserve-YOU JUST STAND AND TRUST YOUR GOD. They will judge you and think that everything you've had to go through should've killed you. BUT WHEN YOU STAND AND THE SMOKE CLEARS, THEY WILL CHANGE THEIR MINDS ABOUT YOU. ONLY A CHILD OF GOD CAN ENDURE SOME OF THE STUFF YOU GO THROUGH. SHOUT HALLELUJAH! WHEN THE TIME COMES, YOU MAKE IT YOUR BUSINESS TO TELL THEM WHO IT IS THAT DELIVERED YOU AND WHO GAVE YOU PEACE IN THE TIME OF TURBULENCE.

QUESTION/CONCLUSION: Is it possible for something that is venomous to bite you without discharging their venom? In other words, can they bite you and hold back their venom? Example: Can a person who is always negative be around without spreading that negative energy? Interesting! I'm open for comments.

CLOSER THAN YOU THINK!

## LIKED/LOVED

In 2 Corinthians chapter 7, Paul wrote a letter to the Corinthians telling them how un-apologetic he was for writing to them in the manner that offended them. It was because of the way in which he wrote the letter that led the Corinthians to change their behavior (REPENT). Look at verse 8, " Even if I caused you sorrow by my letter, I do not regret it. Though I did regret it (past tense)- I see that my letter hurt you, but only for a little while- yet now I am happy, not because you were made sorry, but because your sorrow led you to repentance. For you became sorrowful as God intended and so were not harmed in any way by us.

REVELATION-God allows us free will to live our lives the way we want to but there will come a day when we will have to answer to those decisions and choices.

-If you have the nerve to correct someone when they are misbehaving, be hard-hearted enough to stand your ground. You may be able to see the bigger picture and though you might be exercising tough love, your tough love might lead someone to repentance. Or are you the type of person who needs calamity or sorrowful situations to turn?

-God referred to the Children of Israel as a "stiff-necked people" (Exodus 33:3)

-We should be willing to offend people when we know the bigger picture. Proverbs 27:5 "Open rebuke is better than secret love"

QUESTION: ARE YOU TRYING TO BE LIKED OR ARE YOU TRYING TO BE LOVED?

## YOKED

In 2 Corinthians chapter 6, Paul is addressing the Corinthians on the truth about this walk with Christ. He is doing a compare and contrast between the difficulties of walking with Christ and the victories (verse 1-13). Then from verse 14-18, he tells us to separate ourselves from unbelievers not because we are better than them, but because we don't want to put ourselves in a position that will compromise the faith. (Verse 14) "Do not be yoked together with unbelievers. For what do righteousness and wickedness have in common? Or what fellowship can light have with darkness? What harmony is there between Christ and Belial (Satan)? What does a believer have in common with an unbeliever? What agreement is there between the temple of God and idols?

YOKE - Greek word HETEROZUGIO - and it means to associate discordantly.

REVELATION/UNDERSTANDING- we should be yoked with believers but give an effort to witness to unbelievers. Because we are humans, our natural attraction is to sin. However; when we walk with Christ everyday, w are exercising his principles and standards toward Godly living.

PARABLE: If you go to the gym to work out and exercise, it helps when you have a partner that is just as dedicated than you (if not more). As you exercise together, you get stronger together, maybe not at the same rate of speed, but you get stronger and not weaker. There are going to be some days when you don't feel like going and visa-versa, but you have one another to hold accountable. When you are yoked with someone who doesn't want to go to the gym, they will wear you down until you stop going altogether. Their agenda is very different than yours. It's one thing to have the heart to go and work out, but it's another thing to not want to go to the gym at all. Believers want you to work out or exercise your faith. Nonbelievers don't really care if you work out or not they just want to get their agendas accomplished. Sometimes we are not strong enough YET to not give in to their agendas so Paul is telling us to get around people who think, act and believe as we do, that way we have a better chance to achieve righteous than not.

--If you've recently come out of drinking, you don't want to hang with your bar buddies. If you are married, you want to get with other married couples, (single people shouldn't try to entice you to act like your single when your not). As you walk with Christ, get around people that will enhance your walk and shake the people that will hinder your walk.

Take a goooooooooood look at the people around you and in a NON-judgmental way, calculate what they add to your life and what they take away. Chop Chop!

Have a great day.

## COMFORT

I found something in 2 Corinthians chapter 1 that we should all rejoice about. Whether your going through good or bad times, peaks or valleys, sorrow or bliss, light or darkness. It is not only for the building of your character, but so that you can help someone else out in need. SCRIPTURE (verse 3-4) "Blessed be God, even the Father of our Lord Jesus Christ, the Father of mercies and the God of all comfort; (4) Who comforts us in all our tribulation, that we may be able to comfort them which are in any trouble, by the comfort wherewith we ourselves are comforted by God"

*REVELATION:* Stop griping about what you are going through! The operative words are "GOING THROUGH" and not "STAYING IN". Whatever it is will give you the words to comfort someone else that might go through the same thing in a month or year from now.

-Yes, walking away from an abusive relationship was hard, yes, losing the weight was difficult, yes, changing your spending habits was hard, yes, detaching yourself from leeches was hard, yes, a career change is difficult, yes, being in a long distance relationship can be hard (you can make it)

and YES, walking with God can be very very difficult, but this all qualifies you to help somebody else coming behind you.
PERCEPTION IS EVERYTHING!
"It's not what happens to a person that determines their outcome, it's what the person THINKS about what has happened to them that determines the outcome" (Lafayette Dorsey)

## HAND

Psalm 31 (a Psalm of David). The subtitle in my Bible says "My Times Are In Thy Hand." David spends most of the chapter focusing on how good God has been and how everything God does is by design. (Verse 15) "My times are in thy hand: deliver me from the hand of mine enemies, and from them that persecute me."
--As I thought about hands and what they are used for, the first few things that came to mind was "grabbing" and "holding"
*REVELATION-* God will grab us and He will hold us.
QUESTION-1. Do you acknowledge that YOUR times are in God's hands? 2. Have you committed your life to being in God's hands? 3. Do you believe that being in God's hands is the best place for you? If you answered no to any of these questions but desire to be in God's hands, get somewhere quiet and pray. If you don't know what to say, start by saying "God, I surrender, take my life into your hands."
CONCLUSION- (verse 23-24) "O love the Lord, all ye His saints; for the Lord preserves the faithful, and plentifully rewards the proud doer. Be of Good courage, and He shall strengthen your heart, all ye that hope in the Lord."

## RECOGNIZE A TEST

1Kings 13: 1-34.
HISTORY-This particular chapter focuses on a character whose name is not given but is described as "the man of God".

The man of God was given clear instructions by God to go and prophesy unto the king (Jeroboam). (Jeroboam not only made golden calves for Israel to bow down and
worship, but he also burnt incense and sacrifices to the golden calves upon THE ALTAR OF GOD. Chapter 12:28-32)
EXAMPLE: Emmanuel brought you into his house, fed you, raised you, educated you, and protected you; then you turn around and bring Mr. Chollie into the same house and bow to him, cook for him, brag about him, and make your neighbors come in and bow to him saying, "Mr. Chollie is a great man, look what he has done for me and us."
QUESTION: Is that a slap in the face?
This is equivalent to what happened in the text so God sent a prophet to tell what was going to happen.
CLEAR-The man of God was not only given the words to say to Jeroboam, but was also instructed not to eat, drink, return the same way he came or stay in that place (Chap. 13 verse 8-9). After he (the man of God) did exactly what he was sent to do, he left. He refused the king's proposal and went his way. After he left, somewhere on his journey he stopped to rest and sat under an oak tree (verse 14).
TEST- the Bible says an "old" prophet (verse 11) saddled an ass and chased after the man of God to bring him back to his house. When the "old prophet" caught up with him, he lied to him to get him to go back with him saying, "I am a prophet also as thou art; and an angel spoke unto me by the word of the Lord, saying, Bring back with thee into my house, that he may eat bread and drink water". But he lied to him (verse18).
REVELATION: When God speaks, He is clear. The man of God couldn't recognize a test. The dead give-away was the fact that this prophet asked him to do EXACTLY what God told him NOT to do- WORD FOR WORD. When God speaks to you, don't let people come and distract you. Don't get caught up in their position or title. If God tells you not to do something,

don't do it. If he tells you to go somewhere, go. If He tells you to leave some people, leave them. If He tells you to walk away, walk! We do this all the time in relationships and on our "so-called" jobs. We clearly hear from God, but wait to be validated by peers. People will do all kinds of things "in the name of God" to fulfill their own agenda.

QUESTION- ARE WE ANY GOOD TO GOD BEING HALF OBEDIENT? OUCH! END RESULT- The man of God was eaten by a lion and left on display for everybody to see.

Would you rather be popular and dead, or obedient and live? Recognize a test! Remember, a trap is not designed to look like a trap! Enjoy your day.

## PRIORITIES

I Chronicles 17 and therein was revealed to me two questions. This is a story about king David and how he wanted to show his gratitude to God for all God had done for him, by building Him (God) a house to dwell in. God spoke to Nathan (the prophet) and sent him to David to tell him not to build Him a house because he goes wherever he wants, whenever He wants (verse 5-6).

QUESTION 1: Are you pleasing to God?

QUESTION 2: Do you know what is pleasing to God?

Dr. Luther E. Smith Jr. writes, "The work to which God calls us is with the people whom God seeks to build up. God's priorities must become our priorities. When this happens, our labors serve holy purposes that glorify God and sustain God's people."

## FOLLOW DIRECTIONS

2 Kings chapter 5.

OVERVIEW- In this chapter, Naaman (a man stricken with leprosy) will be healed by God through instructions from Elisha (the prophet). The first thing to note is the fact that Naaman

WASN"T the king, but was considered to be a great man because of what God used him to accomplish. Then the verse goes on to point out "BUT HE WAS A LEPER".

*REVELATION*-1. You don't have to be the one in charge to get recognition. Quit BEING A HATER. If someone else is in position, give them their props but keep it in the right perspective (Mark 12:17-Render to Caesar the things that are Caesar's, but unto God what is God's)---Stop kissing butt trying to get promoted; or worse, trying to make someone else look bad to illuminate yourself! YES YOU! 2.You can be great and be sick at the same time. Don't misunderstand the fact that God will use anybody. Watch how you treat people! Don't judge what's visible on the outside, but focus on the inside, (after all, don't you want people to do that to you)?

3. Naaman never would've known about the prophet had it not been for a "little maid" (verse 2) who served Naaman's wife.

We shouldn't discount a person's wisdom or knowledge based on their job description. We ALL do it or have done it. - Someone has to pick up the trash! Someone has to be the mechanic! Someone has to be the waiter! Someone has to mow the lawn! Someone has to clean the windows! Someone has to do security! THAT DOESN'T MEAN THAT THEY ARE NOT INTELLIGENT. The "little maid" was not only OBSERVANT enough to know the gift that Elisha possessed, but was also WISE enough to know WHEN to ESPOSE him.

We shouldn't be so self-consumed that we ignore the people around us and the gifts they possess! Get to know the people around you, one day God may use you to point them into the right direction to do something great. Hear is a great question to ask! WHAT ARE YOU PASSIONATE ABOUT? WHAT WOULD YOU DO IF YOU KNEW YOU COULDN'T FAIL?

4.Naaman made it to Elisha to be healed but rather than following the instructions that would heal him, he wanted to do something different (look at verse 9-11) "So Naaman came with his horses and with his chariot, and stood at the door of the house of Elisha. (verse 10) And Elisha sent a messenger unto him, saying, Go and wash in Jordan seven times, and thy flesh shall come again to thee, and thou shalt be clean. (v-11) But Naaman was wroth, and went away, and said, Behold "I THOUGHT", he will surely come out to me, and stand, and call on the name of the Lord his God, and strike his hand over the place, and recover the leper". NOTICE-Elisha didn't go, but gave instructions to someone else (a messenger) to give to Naaman. When the message comes from one of God's anointed, do it. Don't focus on the translator. The messenger had a job and did it! 5. You don't need a pastor to lay his/her hands on you or drown you in oil to receive a miracle. We ONLY need to be OBEDIENT!

The Bible says that Naaman went away in rage (v-12).

-Miracles don't always come how WE think! We should be more into Obedience than into Our Opinion!!

-We often come to God with our desires/wants/needs and got the NERVE to tell Him how to do it.

QUESTION- ARE YOU WILLING TO BE EMBARRASED TO GET YOUR MIRACLE? Naaman's healing was in his humility but he didn't want to be embarrassed. He wanted it to be his way. Man/woman of God or not, it will be His way or no way!

Finally- (verse 13) Naaman's SERVANTS were men/women enough to tell him what he NEEDED to hear and not what he WANTED to hear.

QUESTION- ARE THE PEOPLE AROUND YOU AFRAID TO TELL YOU THE TRUTH? ARE YOU AFRAID TO TELL SOME PEOPLE AROUND YOU THE TRUTH?

-Can your employees tell you when your being a jerk without you firing them? Can you tell your employees he/she's being a jerk without you firing them? Can you tell your spouse the truth about themselves and visa-versa?

## FOLLOW DIRECTIONS – PART 2

As I was driving home yesterday, I was thinking about the devotion and two other things came to me. 1. PARTICIPATION- Naaman thought that Elisha (God's Prophet) would " come out to him, stand, and call on the name of the Lord his God, and strike his hand over the place and recover the leper" (2Kings 5:11). God made sure that Naaman PARTICIPATED in the miracle.

--Sometimes we pray for God to heal our bodies, but we won't change our eating habits that made us sick in the first place, nor will we exercise. We ask God to heal our finances, but we won't stop shopping, consuming or even worse, pay our tithes and offering. We'd rather go get a scratch-off. And then have the nerve to ask God to bless us to win. Faith without works is dead (James 2:26).

--Participation makes you a better witness. Participation gives you a greater appreciation. Participation helps you to encourage and strengthen someone else who may need the same miracle. 2. BILLBOARD- God used Naaman as a billboard. God could've healed Naaman with a word, not to mention, stopped him from having leprosy in the first place. God uses us as billboards to lead others to Him. You don't hide a billboard. You put it up as high as you can so everybody can see it.

*REVELATION*-The reason why you are sick in the first place, is so that God can make you a billboard. The reason that you are overweight is so that you will get up, do something about it, and help people who are not yet transformed. The reason why you're going through so much in your marriage is because God is going to use you to help somebody else in theirs. The reason why God took your loved one is because there is still "life after Krogers" and somebody else will need you when they lose their loved one. This whole walk is about

RELATIONSHIP with our Creator. You will make a great billboard.

**LIFE**

Matthew Chapter 7:13-14. And they read (13)"Enter ye in at the strait gate: for wide is the gate and broad is the way, that leadeth to destruction, and MANY there be which go in thereat: (14) Because strait is the gate, and narrow is the way, which leads unto life, and few there be that find it."

*REVELATION/UNDERSTANDING-* Many of us grew up "in the church" and most of the time it was because our parents had to drag us in. Some of us went because we got snacks or candy (that was my reason). Many of us went because there were girls or guys there that we were attracted to. Whatever the case, most of us were there for reasons outside of growing closer to Christ. Then we STRAYED away because RITUAL and Religion only held us for so long! Then as we matured, our motives for going changed. We realized that the world was a cold, cold place and after trying things our way, we realized that we needed to be in church and around church folk.

THE WALK- After we got back "into church" some of us found out that *just* going back to church really wasn't the answer. Nor was the answer memorizing scripture, the books of the Bible or just giving your money. Nor was it singing in the choir, wearing your best outfit that commanded attention or pulling up in a new car so that everybody could see you.

--Once you got back into church, you realized that just being there "physically" was not enough but you had to "PRESS" even further. This is that NARROW GATE Jesus is talking about. Let's look at the word strait- NOT STRAIGHT, but STRAIT which is the GREEK word STENOS- which means Narrow from obstacles standing close about. It's one thing to have to fight your way into church, and another thing to have to fight once you get back in. OBSTACLES-There are many obstacles that hinder us from entering into that narrow strait whether it be Religion, racism, loved ones, ritual or misunderstanding. One of the biggest obstacles is not external but internal. We are born in sin and shaped in iniquity (Psalm 51:5) Please read Hebrews 12:1-3. LIFE- I tagged this devotion LIFE because I have discovered that the Narrow Strait truly does lead to life. Solomon reminds us that everything else is VANITY. ECCLESIASTES Chapters 3,4,5,6,7 (just study the whole book LOL.)

CONCLUSION- Spending time studying, meditating on the Word, and most of all Praying, which are the only ways to become DO-ERS which ultimately lead to TRUE LIFE or LIVING. Which way will you go?

**CHANGE OF HEART**

In John chapter 4, Jesus decides to go against the grain of tradition, and customs by stepping outside of His race, to share love with a Samaritan woman. Jesus knew that it was out of the box to go to Samaria because He told His disciples not to go unto the Gentiles or into any city of the Samaritans (Matthew 10:5) As a matter of fact, He COMMANDED them not to. What is important to note, is the fact that Jesus purposely went to meet her at the well. (verse 4) "And he (Jesus) must needs go through Samaria." (verse 9) "Then saith the woman of Samaria, How is it that thou, being a Jew, askest drink of me, which am a woman of Samaria? for the Jews have no dealings with the Samaritans."

*REVELATION:* LOVE is so powerful that it will make you go against tradition or what is customary. HE CHANGED: Jesus did exactly the opposite of what He told his disciples not to do. He had a change of heart. There are some racist friends and family members that customarily or traditionally think blacks are niggers and whites are crackers and devils. Most of the time, these concepts are passed down from generation to generation. If not by immediate family then by peers or people who are looked up to in the community.

BE OPEN: Pride will often stop us from going deeper in Love. If someone of an opposite race/gender comes with a solution to your problem, don't be so prideful that you miss your blessing or opportunity to go against the grain. It's not just about material either. You have the solution to somebody else's problem, but are to prideful or un-loving to share it. Don't worry about what everybody else thinks about you. Be radical and step outside of normalcy. JESUS knew the perception that the Samaritans had of them (Jews) but PURPOSELY went to change that perception.

-You know how you feel about your boss or how your boss feels about you. You know how you feel about certain co-workers and how they feel about you. You know how certain family members feel about you, and how you feel about them. Do something radical. When you do something radical, somebody WILL have a change of heart (if it is done with the right motive).

**STOP THE BLEEDING**

Judges (21) The Benjamites had been smitten by their brethren (Israel) because of what a few did to the Levite's wife (raped and murdered her). As a result, there were only a few Benjamites that remained because of the slaughter. This led the rest of the children of Israel to try to do whatever they could to help the Benjamites that remained, to find wives so that they would not become extinct.

EXTINCTION-Everyday we watch OUR brothers kill one another and have become completely numb to it. It has become so much apart of the norm, that we have stopped looking for a remedy. We shake our heads and judge the young men with the saggy pants but have not offered ONE single hand to preserve their lives. Not so much as an idea. We are too busy living our lives to be concerned about anybody else. EVEN OUR OWN BRETHREN. If we don't do something, our people will become extinct or have to take wives from other races like the Benjamites. Our men continue to go to jail at alarming rates. Our men continue to fall further and further behind in academics. Our homes continue to be led by women. WHY ARE WE SO AFRAID TO BE GREAT? WHY HAVE WE TURNED A BLIND EYE TO WHAT IS GOING ON IN OUR COMMUNITY? WHAT HAPPENED TO US? The blood of our young men is crying out from the streets. Who is going to stop the bleeding? Please pay attention to Chapter 21 verses 1-5. The children of Israel had accountability so great, that they would put people to death if they didn't go up before the Lord. Not only that, but they came together to worship God on one accord and wept for their brethren. Finally, they asked THE QUESTION? " O Lord God of Israel, Why is this come to pass in Israel, that there should be today one tribe lacking in Israel?"

DO YOU REALLY WANT THE REASONS WHY WE (AFRICAN AMERICANS) ARE IN THE POSITION WE'RE IN?

PLEASE READ LAMENTATIONS CHAPTER 4 AND 5
I'm open to talk because I am diligently searching for answer that will turn us back to Him.

**KEEP TRUSTING**
In Judges chapter 20 we could spend a few days here but I just want to focus on a few key points. UPDATE-The children of Israel were going up to battle against the tribe of Benjamin (yes, their brethren) because some of the men from the tribe of Benjamin raped, abused and eventually murdered the wife of the Levite (she was his concubine). The Levite took his

dead wife home, cut her up into 12 pieces, and sent a piece to each tribe of the children of Israel. All of the tribes of Israel came together to figure out what should be done and it boiled down to BATTLE. FIRST- There IS a time to fight your brethren! Wrong is Wrong and is not exclusive to race, gender, age or even bloodline. If somebody comes into your home and steals something, that person is called a THIEF. It doesn't matter if they are related to you or not. The same goes for this crime against the Levite and his wife. Murder is murder and rape is rape! Look at what the tribes of the children of Israel said (verse 7-9), "Behold, ye are all children of Israel, give here your advice and counsel. (v.8) And all the people arose as one man, saying, We will not any of us go to his tent, neither will we any of us turn to his house. (v.9) but now this shall be the thing which we shall do to Gibeah; we will go up by lot against it." No matter who our family members are, there is a punishment for "folly" which is the Hebrew word Nbalah, literally meaning= crime, wickedness and foolishness. Sometimes we want to protect our loved ones, even when they are wrong. Not So! SECOND-The children of Israel went to battle twice against Benjamin and both times they prayed and received direction from God to go forward. The first day they lost 22,000 men (verse21). The second time they lost 18,000 men (verse 25). What's important for you to understand is the FACT that before the children of Israel went up to battle both times, they asked God if they should go up and He replied yes (verse 18 and verse 23).

QUESTION-What happens when you are obedient to God and you don't get the results you are looking for? God plainly told them to go up to battle. Not only that, but He told them who to send up first (Judah, verse 18).

QUESTION-Have you ever been set up by God? Have you ever felt betrayed by God? Have you ever been disappointed by God? Have you ever looked at the results of a situation and said, "God, this ain't what you promised?"

*REVELATION*-God is in the business of building character, not patronizing. He is more concerned with OUR character than He is with OUR concepts. What will you do when the fire is turned up? Do you remember Shadrach, Meshach and Abednego and what they said right before Nebuchadnezzar threw them into the fiery furnace? (Daniel 3:17-18) "If it be so, our God whom we serve is ABLE to deliver us from the burning fiery furnace, and He will deliver us out of thine hand, O king. BUT "IF NOT", be it known unto thee, O king, that we will not serve thy gods, nor worship the golden image which thou hast set up." CLAUSE- Bishop Noel Jones calls it the "If Not Clause". Will you still serve Him if the outcome isn't what you expected? Will you still trust him if you NEVER get married? Will you still trust Him if you get laid off? Will you still trust Him when your kids are in jail or are acting crazy? Will you still trust Him by paying your tithes when your finances are low? Will you still trust Him to deliver your body from sickness when the conditions seem to be getting worse? Look at what the children of Israel did after losing 40,000 men. (verse 26) "Then ALL the children of Israel, and ALL the people, went up, and came unto the house of God, and wept, and sat there before the Lord, and fasted that day until even, and offered burnt offerings and peace offerings before the Lord. (verse27) And the children of Israel inquired of the Lord (v.28) Shall I YET again go out to battle against the children of Benjamin my brother, or shall I cease? And the Lord said, Go up; for tomorrow I will deliver them into thine hand.

*REVELATION*- God NEVER told the children of Israel that He would deliver them until now (v.28). He never broke His promise because He never made one. He gave them instructions based on their questions. YES they lost some 40,000 men on the way. YES, they were being chased by their

enemies. YES they couldn't understand why God didn't give them victory. YES their obedience caused them heartache. YES it got a bit harder for them to TRUST God every time they felt defeat. BUT- They never stopped seeking God's face or His direction. The children of Israel would go on to defeat their enemies but the point is that God does things in His timing, not ours. The picture is much bigger than we can see. The children of Israel were OBEDIENT. Obedience is what THIS whole life is about. OBEDIENCE!
Will you keep trusting?

## ONE QUESTION

In Judges chapter 17, out of the 13 short verses, one really stood out and it made me ask one question. (verse 6) "In those days there was no king in Israel, but every man did that which was right IN HIS OWN EYES." QUESTION: Who's leading, You or JESUS? When YOU lead, the path is broad and unclear. When Jesus leads, the path is straight and narrow (Matthew 7:14). When YOU lead, you get caught up in sinful situations. When Jesus leads, He directs you away from getting caught up in sinful situations (Psalm 1:1-6). When YOU lead, you stay in a place (job, relationship, community) shorter or longer than you should. When Jesus leads, He moves you at the right time (Proverbs 3:5-6). When YOU lead, you THINK your ways are right. When Jesus leads, you KNOW your path is right (Proverbs 14:12).

Something to chew on!

## SELLOUT

Judges Chapter 16 is a familiar story (Samson and Delilah) but I somehow discovered something fresh. For those of you who are unfamiliar with the story, Samson met Delilah in the valley of Sore (verse 4). Look at verse 5, "And the lords of the

Philistines cam up unto her, and said unto her, Entice him, and see wherein his great strength lieth, and by what means we may prevail against him, that we may bind him to afflict him: and we will give the every one of us eleven hundred pieces of silver."

QUESTION: ARE YOU A SELLOUT? OR ARE YOU BEING SOLD-OUT? Be careful who you choose to love because they may not feel the same way about you. Samson loved this woman, but she clearly didn't love him. Rather than loving him for his strengths, she exploited his weaknesses. She sold him out for some money.

TRUTH: Everybody has weaknesses. Can you trust the person or people closest to you with your weaknesses?

FRIENDSHIP: "I don't judge my friends by what they tell me, I judge them by what I'm able to tell them" (Bishop Noel Jones).

PAY ATTENTION: The signs were there but Samson avoided them. Delilah constantly nagged and tested Samson to find out what his strength was and he ignored them. (verse 16) And it came to pass, when she pressed him daily with her words, and urged him, so that his soul was vexed unto death; (17) that he told her all his heart, and said unto her, There hath not come a razor upon mine head; for I have been a Nazarite unto God from my mother's womb: if I be shaven, then my strength will go from me, and I shall become weak, and be like any other man."

LOOK DEEPER: "be like any other man" There are things about each of us that makes us unique and different. It is those unique qualities that should give us strength to be who God has made us to be. The problem is, WE DON'T RECOGNIZE THEM AS STRENGTHS! You shouldn't want to be like any other man EXCEPT JESUS. QUESTION: Can you appreciate a person who gets more attention? Can you appreciate a co-worker who has good ideas (all the time) without being envious? Can you muster up words to compliment someone who constantly dresses nice? Can you be happy for a person who has a great social life, when yours is not so great?

CURIOSITY: Was Delilah so beautiful that Samson couldn't walk away from her, or was the sex that good? This question is so applicable to some of us today? We are with people for these superficial reasons.

RELEVANCE: There is a TEST for all of us, we may not have met the individual yet, BUT THERE IS A TEST. This is why we should NEVER put a person before God! Only God knows how much we can handle and He will make sure not to give us a HEART for what we can't handle.

EXAMPLE: Some of us have prayed for a certain celebrity to someday be our mates. The flip side is that some of us are so insecure with who we are and our strengths, that we'd drive ourselves crazy wondering where they are or what they are doing throughout the day! LOL

PRAYER- Lord, give me a heart to receive what is good and perfect for me. Give me your eyes that I may not only see the good in the individual but cover their weaknesses. Teach me about my strengths and give me the power to embrace them no matter how small or how great they are. Expose people who don't have my best interest at heart or who will sell me out, as I fulfill my purpose here on earth. When you expose them, give me the strength to take the next step that YOU order me to take. In the name of Jesus I pray, and ask it all. AMEN

## PAST & VOW

Judges Chapter 11 has so much stuff in it that I have to jump right in. It is a story about Jephthah (the son of a harlot) and his relationship with God. (verse 1) Jephthah lived with his father that got married to a woman and had sons by her. The sons sided with one another and drove Jephthah out because they didn't want him to get any of their inheritance, telling him, "(verse 2) thou shalt not inherit in our father's house; for thou art the son of a strange woman."

*REVELATION*: Many of us come from broken homes or have step-siblings. We either have the mother in common, or the father has multiple children by multiple women.

--QUESTION- Do/did you gang up on the "outsider"? or were you the "outsider"? Either way it goes, nobody ASKS to be born, let alone be born into that type of situation. We have a way of making people feel like crap because of something that none of us controls. You DON'T choose siblings and you DON'T choose parents. But you DO choose how you treat people. Some of you need to pick up the phone today and call the sibling(s) that you mistreated. It can make a person's day or change their whole life. WHY? because some of you are the last word and to receive validation from you would mean EVERYTHING to the individual.

--DON'T LET PRIDE STOP YOU FROM CALLING! DON'T LET THE FACT THAT A LOT OF TIME HAS PASSED, STOP YOU FROM CALLING! As a matter of fact, take them out to eat or prepare a meal for them. This interaction may give birth to not only a wonderful relationship, but could also be the key that unlocks either you or their entire future. Speak LIFE and not DEATH!

--As a result of Jephthah being treated like the outsider, he ran away (verse 3) ," Then Jephthah fled from his brethren and dwelt in the land of Tob: and there were gathered VAIN men to Jephthah, and went out with him." That word Vain comes from the Hebrew word REYQ and it literally means-Worthless. Jephthah couldn't get any love at home, so he looked to the streets and found worthless men gathered to him. Sounds like our young men and women. They are not getting the love and attention they need and should be getting at home and end up looking for it in other places. Our young men are joining gangs to get it. Our young women are looking in every car that passes trying to get it. Some of us grew up this way and are STILL trying to get it. The neglect at home turned us away and we've been fighting ever since. In and out of beds. In and out of clubs. In and out of jobs. In and out of relationships.

--My aunt and I were having a conversation Sunday about one of her friends and her children. The mother grew up as an outsider (being of a darker complexion and overweight) than her siblings, and therefore was the outsider. Now one of her daughters is the same way she was ( of a darker complexion and overweight) which has caused the mother to be overprotective of her.

--We are ALL products of our environment. Take the time to look at where you fit in, and how you treated one another or was treated.

--In verse 4, Ammon (enemies) picked a fight with the Children of Israel, who in turn went to fetch Jephthah to come and lead them in battle. Listen to what Jephthah said in verse 7, "Did not ye hate me, and expel me out of my father's house? and why are ye come unto me now when ye are in distress?

--Now they're looking for him. Isn't it funny how those same people that mistreated you turn around and need you! Family! Ain't did nothing to advance your life, but the first time they need something, you get the call. Ain't so-much as called you and said "happy birthday", but need some help with the bills. Expect you to use your resources to help get their children out of trouble!

--WHAT DO YOU DO IF YOU ARE THE OUTSIDER?

Jephthah, made sure that it was worth it for him to come back. In essence, Jephthah put his life on the line to come back and fight because these were still his people. Not only were these his people, but Jephthah had something to prove. Not only to them, but to himself. The moment comes in our lives where we have to look in the mirror and ask, "What have I done with my life?" There are people that we grew up with who we KNEW were gonna go on to be successful. There were also those individuals that we knew wouldn't amount to anything or become VAIN. Then there were those of us who were on the fence. Didn't know how we'd end up! If you have contact now, or know how to get into contact with someone from high school or your old neighborhood, that isn't living up to their potential, reach out to them TODAY and speak life into them.

TESTIMONY-- In June of 1991, my class was set to walk across the stage to receive our diplomas from high school. A very close childhood friend of mine got incarcerated the day before our graduation because he was hanging out with VAIN men and got caught up in an armed robbery. As a result, he served 7 years in prison. I wouldn't see him until 9 years later after returning to Cincinnati (my hometown) to film my first movie "Get Right or Get Left". I had flown home to Cincinnati from Los Angeles to hold auditions during one of my visits, and I saw my childhood friend on the street. When I saw him, we just hugged for at least ten minutes. My heart sobbed for him because he was one of those people who was on the fence, just like me. He said to me, " I heard that you are here to shoot a movie?" I said, "I am". He asked me if he could audition for a part in the movie. In my eyes, he had already had a part in the movie but I invited him to the auditions anyway (I didn't want him to feel like he was receiving a handout). To make a long story short, I gave him a part and he did an excellent job. Although he did an exceptional job in front of the camera, what he said behind the camera changed my life forever. My childhood friend (now a grown man) looked me (another grown man) in my eyes and said, "You restored hope in my life!"

QUESTION-- What else on earth can be more rewarding than a statement like that? Make those calls today and make contact today. Read the rest of Chapter 11 and look at the

VOW Jephthah had to keep! Powerful stuff as it relates to your relationship with God.

**HOW FAR**

You MUST read Judges Chapter 9 for yourself. The story begins at the end of chapter 8 with the returning to evil by the children of Israel, after God had delivered them from their enemies. Abimelech (the son of Gideon's maidservant [not his wife]) persuaded his kinsmen to anoint him king over them. Once he was anointed king, Abimelech went and killed is father's sons (70). Jotham (the youngest brother) is the only one that escaped. ???Are you following men/women of Faith in God or people who are evil, greedy and hungry for the spotlight? Be leery of people that are self-seeking and will stop at nothing to get their way. Be leery of people that will tear others down, to lift themselves up. Be leery of people that are disrespectful to their loved ones. Abimelech literally killed seventy of his own brothers to get his way.

The men of Shechem are just as guilty for not seeing the devil in Abimelech.

COMMON SENSE- If a man/woman is willing to kill his own blood, how will he/she treat you? If a child will disrespect his/her parent, what will they do to you? If a married man/woman will cheat with you, what in the world will make you think that he/she will leave them and be faithful to you?

CONTENTMENT- Jotham (the youngest and only son left) gave the men of Shechem a parable that went like this: (verse 8) "the trees went forth on a time to anoint a king over them; and they said unto the olive tree, Reign thou over us. (9) but the olive tree said unto them, Should I leave my fatness, wherewith by me they honor God and man, and go be promoted over the trees? (10) And the trees said to the FIG tree, come thou, and reign over us. (11) but the fig tree said unto them, should I forsake my sweetness, and my good fruit, and go to be promoted over the trees? (12) then said the trees to the VINE, come thou reign over us (13) and the vine said, should I leave my wine, that cheereth God and man, and go to be promoted over the trees? (14) then said ALL the trees to the bramble, come though and reign over us.

BRAMBLE= Hebrew word ATAD meaning to pierce or make fast; a thorn. I Timothy 6:3-6, "If any man teach otherwise, and consent not to wholesome words, even the words of our Lord Jesus Christ, and to the doctrine which is according to godliness; He is PROUD, knowing nothing, but doting (senile) about questions and strife's of words, whereof cometh envy, strife, railings, evil surmising, Perverse disputing of men of corrupt minds, and destitute of the truth, SUPPOSING THAT GAIN IS GODLINESS: from such withdraw thyself. But GODLINESS with contentment is great gain."

GREED will get you into trouble. What are you working to acquire? What are you trying to achieve? Does your work TRULY involve purpose? Is God leading you, or are you leading yourself? Or worse, are you being led by a FOOL?

Please read this chapter because there is so much content. I'd love to talk about it more in detail if any of you have the time.

## CLICHÉ'

In Psalm 30, I came across a familiar scripture; one that frequent *churchgoers* hear all the time. (Verse 5), "For his anger endures but a moment; in his favor is life: WEEPING MAY ENDURE FOR A NIGHT, BUT JOY COMETH IN THE MORNING." Sometimes as "religious or church folk", we tend to quote scriptures, in particular this one, trying to encourage someone or even ourselves. It has become a cliché' in many cases, just like "blessed and highly favored". Whenever someone is going through something that causes pain, our natural inclination (when we're sincere) is to try to fix their problem, or offer solutions as to how to overcome whatever it is they are going through.

*REVELATION/UNDERSTANDING:* Not everything God allows us to go through warrants a comeback with this scripture. We tend to focus more on "coming out" than we do "being in". What if you get stronger while your in the weeping stage? What if you get a fresh revelation when your in the weeping stage? What if you find your purpose while in the weeping stage? Do we ever take the time to look at the first part of that scripture? Anger! Think about anger for a moment. Have you ever been angry with someone you love? The way you express your anger may be silence, yelling, whipping, taking/repossessing or not doing for etc.. In any case, if you are not bold and just say outright that you are upset or angry with that person, you will do (in most cases) something to let them KNOW that you are angry with them. Somehow, you will bring to their attention that you are angry with them. Is God that way? When He is angry with us, does He cause us to be in a weeping state as a result of something we did to make Him angry? I believe that He does sometimes, but the other times it's solely to build character. I'm so glad that His anger endures but a moment. Please know that "His" moment and "our" moment may be completely different just like "His" night & morning and ours may be completely different. Just remember that when you read or quote these scriptures, be mindful that there just might be another side to WHY this is going on.

## RESTORED

In the 4th and final chapter of Ruth there are so many things that happened but I want to focus on one in particular. Boaz (the wealthy and upright man) marries Ruth and gets her pregnant, and she bares a son. Verse 14-15, "And the women said unto Naomi (the widow who lost her husband and two sons to death), Blessed be the Lord, which hath not left thee this day without a kinsman, that his name may be famous in Israel. And he shall be unto thee a restorer of thy life, and a nourisher of thine old age: for thy daughter-in-law, which loveth thee, which is better to thee than seven sons, hath borne him".

RESTORER= Hebrew Word SHUWB & it means to refresh, relieve, rescue, reverse and recover. Some of us need to be rescued from the hurt that life can bring with it. Naomi fell to the shadow of Ruth and her love story but God saw fit to bless Naomi with a grandson. You never know where or what God will rescue someone from their bitterness or hurt. The child will never be able to replace her other children, nor will it be able to replace the husband she lost, but the child will give her something to look forward to in her old age.

*REVELATION/UNDERSTANDING*-You or your child could be the best blessing that the people around you possess. You never know what a child can do for a broken spirit. Think about your children (if you have any) and who gets joy from seeing them. Make time to see the people, (even if you can't stand them) or take your children by; you never know who you may RESCUE. The birth of the child meant that Naomi wouldn't have as much time to reflect on what she didn't have, but instead of what she did.

**THERE IS LIFE AFTER KROGERS**
Let's take a look at Ruth chapter 1. I will start out by stating that, "in order for some things to begin, some things must end. In order for some things to live, some things must die". There was a famine in the land of Bethlehem so Elimelech (Naomi's husband) took his wife and two sons to Moab. While in Moab, Elimelech died so it was Naomi and her two sons left. The two sons each took wives in Moab and lived there for about ten

years. After which, her two sons died also. Naomi was left with two daughters-in-law. Naomi decided that it was time to leave Moab and return home to Bethlehem THINKING that she had nothing. She sent her two daughters-in-law away stating that she had nothing else to offer them (v.8-13). One of the daughters left but the other stayed and nothing but death would separate them (v.16-18).

REVELATION/UNDERSTANDING: When you have been with people or in a particular place for so long, that place or those people become the ingredients that make up your life. What happens when someone suddenly dies? What happens when someone walks away from you? What happens when you have to move out of your habitat and totally relocate? What happens when a company lays you off after you've dedicated years of your life there? Someone close to me recently (in the past two years) was divorced by her husband of 30+ years. He was abusive to her in many ways, but she stayed and she loved him with every since of her being? People around her couldn't understand why she hurt so bad for a man that treated her so bad. Part of her hurt was because she felt used, having gave her all only for him to walk out on her (for another woman who happened to be Caucasian and was the same age as their daughter). The other part of her hurt was because she was now alone, left with three grown kids and two grandchildren. She felt like she should be in the final stretch of life where she'd enjoy retirement with her husband and spend time with their grandchildren. Instead, she works two jobs to make ends meet and hardly gets a chance to see her grandchildren. She would cry herself to sleep and often call me crying her eyes out. Why wouldn't she, her life changed forever overnight! Over time, you learn how to blend into your environment and just when you get comfortable, God finds a way to upset your circumstances. Naomi was in this place. She felt like she had nothing to offer her daughters-in-law let alone anybody else. She felt like she could just crawl up under a rock and die. Alicia (my friend) decided to write a book about her experiences. One night she called me overjoyed with the idea and as we talked, she stumbled upon names for a few of her chapters. One of which being, "There Is Life After Kroger's". She had been ritualistically going to Kroger's (grocery store) for 30+ years to shop for her family of five.

Now she would have to learn how to shop, cook, prepare and live for herself. Today I just want to encourage someone. Whatever you just went through, are in the midst of, or heading into, keep in mind that God is interested in building character and in order for some things to live, some things must die, and in order for some things to begin, some things must end. The death of Alicia's marriage gave birth to her unwavering relationship with the Lord, and new opportunities to live HER DREAMS. In her words, "I'll do whatever I have to do, in order to follow the Lord". Read the chapter for yourself and remember, There is LIFE after Kroger's!!!!

## LIFE AFTER KROGERS – PART 2

In Ruth chapter 3 there are two things I want you to observe. The first pertains to Naomi (Ruth's mother-in-law). Remember back in chapter 1 how Naomi was broke up over the loss of her husband and children and as a result, she felt her life to be useless? Not only that, but she tried to send Ruth and her sister away, because she thought she had nothing else to offer them. Well now here we are in chapter 3 and Naomi's second life is taking effect.

*REVELATION/UNDERSTANDING*-Interpretation is everything. Naomi is using her wisdom to teach Ruth about men and how to approach them. I know some of you are "old-fashioned" and feel like you need to be pursued, but Naomi has been through a lot and has wisdom in this area. The life after Kroger's is taking effect. If you've been through something (especially something catastrophic) most of the time its not just for you, but for someone coming after you. God puts us through some things in order to build character and to share what we went through in order to be a blessing to others. EXAMPLE: How are you going to help someone overcome their fight with drug addiction, if you've never been a drug addict?

*REVELATION/UNDERSTANDING-* (verse 3-4) Ruth got the instructions from Naomi about what to do once she got to Boaz. Boaz had been drinking at dinner and his heart became merry (slightly intoxicated). Ruth was sent to UNCOVER his feet, NOT sleep with him. You do not have to connive, manipulate, or take advantage of someone because they are in a vulnerable state. So what you gave someone some money, that doesn't mean use that to gain an advantage. And if someone did give you something, make sure it doesn't become a handcuff. You do not have to subject yourself to someone because they appear to have "more power" than you do. You do not have to sleep with your boss, because you want a promotion. And BOSSES, you shouldn't take advantage of the fact that you are a boss and that you COULD sleep with people or take advantage of people just on that fact alone. BOAZ was rich and ruled over much but he DID NOT use his power to take advantage of Ruth. STOP being manipulative, you don't have to do it. Listen to what Boaz says to Ruth (even being intoxicated), verse 10-11 "Blessed be thou of the Lord, my daughter: for thou hast shown more KINDNESS in the latter end than at the beginning, inasmuch as thou follows not young men, WHETHER POOR OR RICH. And now my daughter, fear not; I will do to thee ALL that thou requires: for ALL the city of my people doth know that thou art a virtuous woman."

--When your light is shining, everybody knows it. You may not think so or even acknowledge it but it is true. Be and stay true to yourself and to God, HE will make people bless you. Grace and Peace!

**PAY ATTENTION**

In Joshua chapter 23, Joshua (who is well stricken in age or waxed old) has called all of Israel together to summarize what God has done for them and to remind them of how to continue in their obedience, so that they will continue to be blessed and led by God. (Verse 8-13) "But cleave unto the Lord your God, as ye have done unto this day. For the Lord hath driven out from before you great nations and strong: but as for you, no man hath been able to stand before you unto this day. One man of you shall chase a thousand: for the Lord your God, He it is that fights for you, as he hath promised you. (Verse 11) Take good heed therefore unto yourselves, that ye love the Lord your God. Else if ye do in any wise go back, and cleave unto the remnant of these nations. Even these that remain among you, and shall make marriages with them, and go in unto them, and they to you: Know for a certainty that the Lord your God will no more drive out any of these nations from before you; but the shall be snares and traps unto you, and scourges in your sides, and thorns in your eyes, until ye perish from off this good land which the Lord your God hath given you".

CLEAVE= Hebrew word DABAQ and it means to: catch by pursuit, -abide fast, cleave (fast together) FOLLOW CLOSE (hard after), be joined (together). Have you ever been in a car following behind someone because they knew the directions and you didn't? You have to pay close attention to their vehicle because sometimes cars may come between you, or the person whom you are following may have to suddenly accelerate to get to a spot or come to a sudden stop to avoid an accident. Sometimes the person has gotten way ahead of you so they put on their hazard lights so that you can find them (especially at night). Finally, you are not the only one following them, but have others in a car or cars following you.

UNDERSTANDING/REVELATION- God is the one with the directions so do whatever you have to do to stay with the one with the directions. You can't even let people (cars) get over in between you sometimes because they will cause you to lose your leader. They don't know or care that you are following someone. They just want to get over at your expense. Then there are times when people "BOGART" their way into your lane (life) because of their persistence. They are even willing to hit you to get into your lane.

DON'T LET PEOPLE BOGART THEIR WAY INTO YOUR LIFE BECAUSE OF THEIR PERSISTENCE (LADIES). IF THEY WANT TO BE WITH YOU BAD ENOUGH, THEY WILL TAKE THE TIME TO PAY ATTENTION TO YOU LONG ENOUGH TO KNOW THAT YOU ARE FOLLOWING SOMEONE, AND GET BEHIND YOU. Not only that, but when they realize who you are following, they will make sure that you will stay with that leader. (Say you catch a flat or need to pull over to refuel, that person will go up ahead and alert the person you are following to the attention you need). But if they don't pay attention long enough to your signals, they won't know who you are following. Don't take a cell phone break, because the moment you look away, you could lose your leader. He may make a sudden turn or TAKE a detour, or even worse, stop on a dime. He stopped, but you keep going.

CATASTROPHY. Now you are leading your own way. HOW CATASTROPHIC!!! Then there are times when the person you are following may make a traffic light and you got stuck, or you are on the expressway and they have gotten way out in front of you so they put on their hazard lights. Those hazard lights represent relocation.

LEADERSHIP- A good leader always pulls over to take time to wait for you, or to go back and get you. I'm so glad that God

always has on His hazard lights. Whenever we get behind, He knows it. Whenever we need to refuel, He knows it. Whenever we have a flat and can no longer go on until we CHANGE it, He knows it. Even those of us who are in leadership and have others following us, God knows and alerts us that something isn't right with someone behind us. Either they have gotten to far behind, need to refuel, or have a flat of their own.
DON'T FOOL YOURSELF- If you act like you don't want to CHANGE your flat, He will wave the other people around you.

## FIGHT – PART 2

This was breaking news for me as I left my home and got into my car and headed to my destination. Earlier I mentioned how the (verse 47)"children of Dan went to go and fight against Lechem, and took it, and smote it with the edge of the sword, and possessed it, and dwelt therein, and called Leshem, Dan, after the name of Dan their father".

*REVELATION-* I pondered on how the people of Lechem were murdered and how their land had been possessed by the children of Dan. I concluded that God has people and situations already setup for you to conquer. YES! Some people are ONLY in position to be conquered by God's people. He even told Pharaoh in Exodus 9:16 and again in Romans 9:17 "for this cause have I raised thee up, that I might show my power in thee, and that my name might be declared throughout all the earth". In other words, HE will create a situation to give you a revelation and call it Jehovah Jireh (my provider). I couldn't feel sorry for Lechem after that because I understand that when you are on GODS' side, you put the enemy under your feet. I'm not saying you kill people, but understand this one thing, and that's the fact that if there was no CEO in the first place, how are you gonna obtain that position if God showed it to you? David was the first man in the second position (as Bishop Noel Jones states). When

David was given the promise, somebody else was in the position. One of three things have to happen in order for that promise to come to pass: either Saul has to die off, has to resign, or has to be overtaken. We all know he wasn't gonna resign, and who is gonna wait another fifty years for someone to die? What's left?
FIGHT good people! FIGHT!

**WHAT ARE YOU WAITING FOR**
I found myself stuck in Joshua chapter 18 verse 3 which reads, "And Joshua said unto the children of Israel, how long are ye slack to go to possess the land, which the Lord God of your fathers hath given you"? There were still seven tribes that had not received their inheritance and Joshua is on their case for being lazy about getting what was promised to them.
*REVELATION/UNDERSTANDING*: These seven tribes that had not yet received their inheritance just came out of the wilderness so maybe they didn't know HOW to possess their inheritance. It seems like they should be so hungry to get out on their own and make some things happen for their families but the reality of the matter is that they were either AFRAID of possessing or fighting for their inheritance or they didn't understand what it meant to be FREE. Have you ever wanted something for somebody so bad but they didn't want it for themselves? Don't get comfortable with being uncomfortable! For most of us it's our jobs. I heard an acronym for JOB and it means JUST OVER BROKE. This system has a way of controlling you and making you believe that without a job you can't make it. You can make it if you WORK. It is very difficult to break cycles of poverty when this is all that a person has been accustomed to. There are some first, second and even third generation prison and welfare recipients due to the fact that they had never seen anybody else get an education or go out to work. Only GOD can take us from nothing to

something. The Hebrew word for slack is- Raphah and it literally means 'fail, faint, be feeble, forsake, idle, leave, let alone, be still, be slothful, and be weak'. What will it take for you to possess your inheritance? GO GET IT! IT'S YOURS. What are you waiting for?

The land was subdued (verse 1) or- KABASH which is HEBREW meaning - to conquer, bring into bondage, keep under, bring into subjection. You have been given an inheritance, ask GOD for counsel on how to POSSESS it? Go get it!

## HEART

In Joshua chapter 14, land is still being distributed to the remaining Children of Israel who had not yet received their inheritance. verse 2 jumps right in and tells us how the land was distributed and who ordered it to be so. verse 2,"By LOT was their inheritance, as the Lord commanded by the hand of Moses, for the nine tribes, and for the half". The Hebrew word for LOT is 'goral' and it simply means- a portion or destiny. Some of you can't help it, it is your destiny to be blessed. verse 6-8 made me shout. Caleb (remember him) had not yet received his inheritance and did not hesitate to come forward to remind Joshua about God's promise to him while Moses was in leadership. One important note was the fact that Caleb waited until it was his tribes' turn to receive their inheritance. In other words, he didn't try to step on anybody else's toes (any of the other tribes) when they were getting blessed. When you know what God promised YOU, you don't have to be jealous of what other people get. If you haven't received a promise from God, maybe its because you want what He has to give but don't want Him, maybe it's because your leadership hasn't taught you how to hear God's agenda for your life but instead to hear theirs, maybe you heard a promise from God but because it was so big and out of your realm to complete on your own, you gave up and thought yourself to be crazy; then you really thought the promise was crazy when you shared it with people of no faith, or maybe you put down your promise and picked up "the American Dream" and as a result you haven't had time to Rest or Reflect on your promise.

Look at verse 7 and 8, "Forty years old was I when Moses the servant of the Lord sent me from Kadesh-barnea to espy out the land; and I brought him word again as it was in MINE HEART (he's talking about the book of Numbers Chapter 13 verses 25-33). (Verse 8) "Nevertheless my brethren that went up with me made the heart of the people melt: but I wholly followed the Lord My God". At the age of 40, Caleb was sent With eleven other spies (each representing a tribe from the Children of Israel) and they all observed the same thing but had different interpretations. (God I feel your help coming).

You might have the same job or position as some people, you might share the same responsibilities, you might be under the same authority, you might come from the same family, you may even go to the same church, BUT what kind of HEART do you have? Caleb had the heart of a man who Knew and Trusted in His God. This wasn't speculation. Caleb Knew that God would fight their battles and that they would win, however; his fellow spies "made the hearts of the people to melt".

What's even more powerful is the fact that the people who's hearts melted, didn't see the land for themselves but grew afraid based on what other people said.

-WATCH HOW YOU TALK TO PEOPLE. YOU CAN EITHER SPEAK LIFE AND ENCOURAGE THEM TO PURSUE THEIR PROMISE OR SPEAK DEATH AND PRONOUNCE THE BENEDICTION ON THEIR PROMISE.

verse 10- Caleb was forty (40) at the time God gave him the promise of his land and he is now eighty-five (85). Listen to his words. "the Lord has kept me alive, as he said, these forty five years, even since the Lord spake this word unto Moses, while the Children of Israel wandered in the wilderness: and now lo, I am this day fourscore and five years old. As yet I am as STRONG this day as I was in the day that Moses sent me: as my strength was then, even so is my strength now, for war, both to go out, and to come in. Now therefore give me this MOUNTAINM whereof the Lord spake in that day; for thou heardest in that day how the Anakims were there, and that the cities were great and fenced: if so be the Lord WILL be with me, then I SHALL be able to drive them out, as the Lord SAID".

*REVELATION/UNDERSTANDING-* God keeps promises. God preserves you to enjoy your promises. Don't give up. Caleb asked for the whole mountain, not an apartment. In other words, quit insulting God by asking for stuff you can get on your own! Anybody can get a man or woman, but only God can give a man or woman who will help you to fulfill the promise and purpose He gave you (notice I didn't say a Perfect person, earning 7 figures who looks like Denzel or Halle Berry with more Degrees than a thermometer, with perfect credit and has no children). LOL Caleb's statement about taking the land, even if the Anakims were there reminds us that he has the HEART of a champion and the FAITH of a man who KNOWS his God. What kind of heart do you have? Until we meet or speak again, may your Heart pump courage and not kool-aid as you decide TODAY that you will fight with everything inside of you to fulfill your promise. Have a Caleb attitudinal day.

**REFLECTION**

I want to call your attention to Joshua chapter 12 verses 6 & 7. verse 1-6 reflects on the Children of Israel and the kings they defeated and the land they possessed under Moses leadership and verse 7-24 reflects on the kings they defeated and land they possessed under Joshua's leadership.

*REVELATION/UNDERSTANDING-* The last verse in chapter 11 says, " And the land rested from war". The entire Chapter 12 is dedicated to reflecting on the Children of Israel's' victories. Look at the leadership in your life. There should be a path of victories that you should be able to reflect on. Though the Children of Israel complained and sometimes doubted, they still had enough sense to follow leadership that produced fruit. PARENTS- when you are obedient and following God, your children have no choice but to be blessed and have victory. The rest we receive after being in battle is just that REST. In that REST, REFLECT because that will be your ammunition and re-assurance that God will bring you through your next battle. TESTIMONY- A few years back, I moved to California from Ohio by myself at the age of 25 (I had about $400 in my pocket at the time). Without ANY training, education, background, exposure or even desire for the arts or filmmaking, God used me to write and direct a feature length movie entitled "Get Right or Get Left". I shot the film in Ohio and everything I needed when was provided for me by total strangers as soon as I got off the plane. I'll make a long story short by stating that I know at least 4 people who walked on faith as a result of me walking on faith. All are from Ohio and three of the four followed my footsteps and moved to Los Angeles. One was working in a hair salon owned by the comedian Monique and recently got married, One is working in production for a show called "The Biggest Loser", one currently travels around the world as a motivational speaker and the other is living in Atlanta and is working for a man named Tyler Perry. Your leadership by example aught to produce fruit. (NOT EVERYBODY IS A PULPIT PREACHER)

SIGNIFICANCE- I am in pre-production for a feature film entitled "We Must Go Forward vol.1 The Blueprint" set for production July 10th. I don't know where the money or personnel will come from, but I'm CERTAIN that it will come. I've both RESTED & REFLECTED which gives me the faith and stamina to fight. This is a testament to all of you as witnesses. My budget came back at $5 million and I don't have the money yet. I'm exactly one month away from shooting and to date I have hired one person. This is not only a testament that this film will get made, but also to the fact that fruit will be produced as a result. Other people will believe in Jesus Christ who don't yet believe and those who do, will be stronger believers. Until we meet or speak again, may you Rest and Reflect on your past victories and have the courage to break away from leadership that isn't producing victory in your life.

**HARD**
Joshua chapters 10 and 11 talk about the Children of Israel's victories over kings in the north and south parts of their promised land. There were kings who heard about Joshua and the Children of Israel's battles and victories and therefore tried to build alliances with other kings and their armies to fight against them. It never worked. I'd like to call your attention to two verses. Chapter 11 verse 20 and verse 23. verse 11 "For it was of the Lord to harden their hearts, that they should come against Israel in battle, that he might destroy them utterly, and that they might have no favor, but that he might destroy them, as the Lord commanded Moses.
*REVELATION/UNDERSTANDING-* Have you ever had a boss, family member or someone come against you for no apparent reason? Sometimes God has to induce or "harden" people to come against you because you are too easy-going and you don't want to cause any ripples. Or maybe your season has expired at a particular place or with a particular person or group of people but you are to COMFORTABLE to leave on your own. Bottom-line, since you WON'T pick a fight,

God will pick one for you, not for any other reason except to show you who HE is and that HE will fight your battles. Hebrews 11:6 says, "it is impossible to please God without Faith".

Chapter 11:23, closes with the sentence, "And the land rested from war". Someone has been fighting for a long time and have grown weary. Be mindful of WHAT and WHY you are fighting because we can fight the wrong battles and wonder why we haven't had victory. God will give you rest when you fight the battles HE put before you. We sometimes create battles that are unnecessary which causes us heartache, stress, and unhappiness. Ask God to remove people, jobs and situations from your life that go against His plan for you and watch what happens. Be careful not to try to keep those people, jobs and situations in your life after HE shows you that you or them must go. When the right battle is chosen for you, HE will give you rest at the appointed time. May you have the courage to receive this word and step out on God today and not retreat until He gives you rest.

**NEW DAY**

In Joshua Chapter 5 the children of Israel had crossed over into the Promised Land but there were a few things that happened that were very significant. verse (4-5) One of them was the fact that Joshua was commanded to circumcise the people because "this group" were BORN in the wilderness while those who started the journey had died as a result of their disobedience (verse 6). Then God told Joshua that (verse 9) this was the day that He rolled the reproach of Egypt from off of them. Then finally in verse 11, even though they were in the Promised Land, they still ate the old food one last time before they ate of the fruit of the land. This is my revelation as it related to the text. (Verse 4-5), Some of us were born in this wilderness and it wasn't our fault for the sins of our forefathers but we have to make the decision right here to get on one accord so that we don't repeat past mistakes by worshipping false images and being disobedient. Furthermore, we aught to educate one another about our history of what was done because the fact that we were BORN into this particular time and set of circumstances, we can't fully appreciate what we have and the PROPER perspective it should be placed in. (Verse 9) - There was a beginning to Israel's reproach and there was an ending. We can move into the Green with God if we get and stay on one accord. We simply need to check our priorities. (Verse 11) - Before we continue to eat the good of the land, we should be mindful and grateful daily of the sacrifices that were made and more importantly, how God is merciful to us. I know that some of us can afford to eat out every day but every now and then we may need to eat some beans and cornbread or some Ramen Noodles. Not only that, but we may need to go and buy someone who we KNOW can't afford to not only eat out every day or once in a while, but also those individuals who are wandering the streets hungry. You never know how much a meal and a conversation can CHANGE a life. May your day be filled with love and light and may your heart be pricked to love as Christ loved.

**PERSPECTIVE**

Luke Chapter 20. Look at what Jesus says to some spies sent by the chief priests and scribes. They asked Him this question (verse 22) "Is it lawful for us to give tribute unto Caesar, or no? (v.23) But He perceived their craftiness, and said unto them, "Why tempt ye me? (v.24) Show me a penny. Whose image and superscription hath it?" They answered and said, Caesar's. (v.25) And He said unto them, "Render unto Caesar the things which be Caesar's, and unto God the things which be God's."

REVELATION/UNDERSTANDING: Your boss may employ you to do a job, but that doesn't mean that they have the right to do any and everything they want to you. You must decide what those limits are. They don't decide the limits, you do.
-What do you stand for? What WON'T you tolerate?
-Some of us get caught up because we don't FULLY understand our job description. Then we end up mad when our day has been spent and we didn't get a chance to do what we needed/wanted to get done for ourselves or our families.
-Don't allow folk to manipulate you because they may have SOME authority over you.
--I remember watching an interview that the media was conducting against the basketball player Chris Webber. In the interview, they were asking him questions pertaining to his private life off of the court. He told them in so many words "I play basketball for ya'll, everything else is none of your business!"
-Sometimes people will try to control you.
Jesus is telling the spies that Caesar's face being on the money doesn't mean anything more than that.
-You use the money to buy things. You don't BOW to or WORSHIP the money. You use it!
STOP, putting your boss before YOUR family! Put things back in the right Perspective.
--The spies were trying to set Jesus up to make a fool of Him or to get Him to contradict Himself. It's a control mechanism.
--Watch some of your co-workers, some of them think their your boss too. Naw, their just your co-worker. The job description may be different, but they are not your head. Respect them for their role in the whole scheme of things, but don't be taken advantage of.

## FRONT STREET

Galatians Chapter 2. (verse 11) "When Peter came to Antioch, I opposed him to his face, because he was clearly in the wrong. (12) Before certain men came from Ames, he USED to eat with the Gentiles. But when they arrived, he began to draw back and separate himself from the Gentiles because he was afraid of those who belonged to the circumcision group.

--Don't get brand new when you get around the workplace.

Some of us act one way when we're around church folk but when we get around our friends, its a different story. While we are around church folk, everything is "praise the lord, hallelujah" but immediately after church some of us get to cussing (cursing for some proper folk), drinking, smoking, backbiting, gossiping, shacking and but of course, laying-up.

-We shouldn't portray to be one way and act completely opposite when non-believers come around. Peter was afraid that the unbelievers would do something to him so he acted like the Jews when the Jews came around. He was a Jew by birth but acted as a Gentile until some Jews came around.

--You don't have to try to fit in. YOU CAN'T! YOU STAND OUT! Because it's the Christ in you. IT'S NOT YOU! IT'S THE CHRIST IN YOU THAT MAKES YOU STAND OUT. (verse 20) "I have been crucified with Christ and I NO LONGER LIVE, but CHRIST lives in me.

-You stand out on your job, that's why their messing with you. You stand out and you stand up for Christ and His people, that's why you offend some people. You've got more courage in your toe than most people have in their entire bodies. Don't jeopardize that because you make some people uncomfortable. Your not supposed to fit in.

PARABLE- I wear a size 14 shoe. Don't buy me a size 12 because it doesn't fit. When you try to fit into something that's too small, you get corns (some of ya'lls feet are jacked up now

so you know what I'm saying). Whenever you try to fit into a space that's to small for you, it's going to hurt.
-Does it make more sense for someone to buy me a size 15 so that I can grow into it? Get around people that make you grow. Please read the chapter, we could be here all day.
ASSIGNMENT-try to find out what Peter was so afraid of; also what true liberation means.

## ONE MAJOR GIFT

Galatians chapter 1. One of the greatest gifts that a person can receive from God is deliverance from the opinions of other people. Some of us grew up under people or associate with people who have such a strong hold on our minds that our decision making is predicated on what we believe they would think about the move we are/were contemplating making.
-To this day, many of us had dreams we wanted to pursue but didn't because of what people said.
-Many of us wouldn't date certain people because of what people said.
-Many of us wouldn't go to the college of OUR dreams because of what others thought about it.
-Many of us refused to do things different (even though it ate us up inside) but instead went along with tradition.
-Many of us wouldn't change religions because of what some people MIGHT say.
Let's look at verse 10, "Am I now trying to win the approval of men, or of God? Or am I trying to please men? If I were STILL trying to please men, I would not be a servant of Christ."
If you will take up your cross and follow Christ, He Will give you the deliverance from people that you need to pursue your passion and purpose. Paul goes on to talk about the way he used to believe and the things he used to do that went against Christianity. He then makes a statement as such to let his readers know that he was clear about a few things.

1. He was clear about who he used to be and who he had become.
2. He was clear about who called him and who he belonged to.
3. He was clear about his mission.

QUESTION: If you had clarity about these three things in your life, how much more productive could you be?

God has a way of liberating us to do His will. Are all of us preachers?

NO! Are all of us CEO's? NO! Are all of us evangelists? NO! Will all of us be rich and/or famous? NO! Are you still trying to please people or have you made up your mind that you will please God? Have you been delivered from people or are there still some people whose opinion you FEAR?

CLOSING THOUGHT- You can please people and NOT please God, but you cannot please God and NOT please God's people!

Closer than you think!

## RELAX

In 2 Corinthians chapter 10, Paul defends his authority in the ministry but he is defending it against the people who he have already converted to believing in Christ. His rationale was that he understood having to fight and display boldness with non-believers, but he shouldn't have to be that way with believers.

(verse 1-2) "By the meekness and gentleness of Christ, I appeal to you-I, Paul, who am "timid" when face to face with you, but "bold" when away! I beg you that when I come I may not have to be as bold as I expect to be toward some people who think that we live by the standards of this world.

-When we become believers, we sometimes have the tendency to make other believers feel like every word, sentence or quote has to be something to do with church, the Bible, or the typical clichés "blessed and highly favored, anointed for the appointment, hallelujah, thank you Jesus" or feel that we have to carry around a 50 pound Bible.

RELAX- Paul is saying that he just wants to relax when he gets around his spiritual family. Not that he can start sinning or doing whatever he pleases, but he shouldn't have to come home from WORK only to have to keep WORKING.

He literally begs them to understand that he is who he says he is and just because he displays meekness or humility around his folks, doesn't mean he's soft or less spiritual.

QUESTION-Do some people see you as "mean" because of your position? Do some people see you as a pushover because of your position? There is enough to fight everyday you walk out your door, should you have to fight once you re-enter it?

-The people who are closest to you should know you the best but this is not always the case. Have you ever been with someone for a long period of time only to find out that they don't know you at all? Or you don't know them?

SOLUTION-Just let your light shine. When you walk with Christ, people will see it. Don't let people bait you into proving your relationship with God by words, your actions will speak much louder.

ONE LAST NOTE: Believers have difficult days as well so don't be surprised if you ask a person in the body how their day was and the reply "horrible". We all have challenging days. Some people will constantly ask how your day was, not because they really care, but because they hope it was as miserable as theirs. And they want to see (after they know the day was challenging) if your still going to say what you normally say. 'll be here all day if I don't go. Have a wonderful day.

**WATCH THE PERKS**

Chapter 18 of I Samuel is filled with lessons.

-We pick it up right after David has slain Goliath and the men are returning home from the battle. (verse 6&7) The WOMEN came out from all the towns of Israel to MEET KING SAUL with singing and dancing, with joyful songs and with tambourines and lutes. As they danced they sang, "Saul has slain his thousands, and David his tens of thousands." (Verse 8) Saul was very angry; this refrain galled him. "They have credited David with tens of thousands, " he thought, "but me with ONLY thousands. What more can he get but the kingdom?" (Verse 9) and from that moment on, Saul kept a Jealous eye on David.

*REVELATION/UNDERSTANDING*: Gotta be wise (especially you women) of how you talk to people (men in general especially those who are in position.

--Men are often very egotistical and the right "wrong" words at the right wrong time can make YOUR life a living hell.

-It doesn't matter who has the position, what matters is who has the POWER!

-Some years ago, Bishop Noel Jones preached from this chapter and subtitled the lesson: "First, In a Second Position"

--When you have the power, who needs the position or title? The Bible says in verse 14, "In everything David did he had great success because the Lord was with him." (v 15) When Saul saw how successful David was, he was afraid of him. (v. 16) BUT ALL ISRAEL and JUDAH LOVED DAVID, because he led them in their campaigns.

--You may not be the head of a church. You may not be the CEO of the company. You may not be the Principal of your school. You may not be the Manager on your job. You may not even be Partner at your firm. But the POWER is not in the position, the POWER is in the anointing.

-People love and respect you because of the light you are TO THEM. You may NEVER be the CEO, Principal, Manager, Supervisor, lead Pastor or Partner, but you are a leader.

--People fear you, not because you carry a pistol, not because you know more than them (sometimes), not because you have the most money, but because of the GOD in you.

NOTICE****** David was WISE!! PLEASE BE CAREFUL NOT TO EAT FROM PHAROAH'S TABLE!!! YOU MUST & I REPEAT MUST, WATCH WHAT YOU ACCEPT FROM PHAROAH.

-Just because you do a good deed or step out of the box to make things better, doesn't mean you need to accept everything that is offered to you as a result. Sometimes when you accept that position, you can't say the things you used to be able to say. Sometimes they RAISE you up to SHUT you up. Not because you are doing a heck of a job, they are trying to keep you close to steal your ideas or control your INFLUENCE.

--(Verse 17) Saul tried to give David his daughter to marry in an effort to make him think that he was now loved by Saul.

--Don't you know that people will SACRIFICE their own children to satisfy their own evil ways!!! I hope you are not one of those people.

CONCLUSION:

1. Just work hard and do what you can. If God wants you there, He'll put you there.

2. Don't get caught up in titles. Get caught up in anointing. Observe the people around you and get with people who have favor on their life.

3. Don't be jealous or envious toward someone; especially to someone that God is blessing. Do whatever you can to be a blessing to them because if you do it with the right motive, the blessings will fall on you as well.

4. AND MOST IMPORTANT: Don't apologize for what God has done for you. Don't try to hide because He has used you to do something great, but be WISE in how you handle your

anointing. If people can't handle your anointing, that's their fault. Don't make yourself a hermit because other people can't handle your anointing. Just be careful of how you handle people. You still have people to lead!

## R U LIVING OR EXISTING

Questions: 1. Are you living or existing? 2. If someone pushed you in the water would you swim? 3. Are you playing Offense or Defense? Statements: I need a new job! I want to write! Anything is possible! Ladies and gentlemen, do we really have faith or are we playing? Or, are we REALLY as fed up as we say we are? Stop cheating yourself AND the people who NEED to see you step out and LIVE! I know you don't have the audacity to think staying on a job for 40 years is why God created you.

Conclusion: I found that most people I talk to aren't dying to LIVE, but instead living to die!

## DON'T LOSE SIGHT

I Kings chapter 6. This entire chapter is dedicated to providing the details of the temple that Solomon was building for the Lord - everything from materials that were being used, down to the flowers that would dress the place. Even in the midst of such detail the most important part of this chapter wasn't the temple itself but is seen here in verse 11-13 (11) The word of the Lord came to Solomon: (v.12) "As for this temple you are building, if you follow my decrees, carry out my regulations and keep all my commands and obey them, I will fulfill through you the promise I gave David your father. (v.13) And I will live among the Israelites and will not abandon my people Israel."

*REVELATION/UNDERSTANDING*: God is more concerned with how we live than what we have or achieve.

-God reminded Solomon in the MIDST of what he was doing of how he should live.

-In the midst of what you are doing, don't lose sight of God and what He requires from you! I know that you get busy at times, but don't Lose Sight of the big picture! We oftentimes think that

because we are doing something "for God" or for "good" that it gives us a pass to conduct ourselves in any way we please. We use "our righteousness or good deeds" to green light our backsliding or unrighteousness. In the midst of what you are doing, DON'T LOSE SIGHT!
Play Offense!

**WHAT'S FOR YOU IS FOR YOU**
I Kings chapter 1. In this chapter, King David is on his deathbed and now has to anoint someone to take his place. One of his sons (Adonijah) took it upon himself to make himself the king. He got all of his friends together, gathered together the people, made a feast and even sacrificed cattle, calves and sheep; trying to make himself ruler in David's stead.
REVELATION/UNDERSTANDING: Don't raise yourself up! Let other people in position raise you up.
2. No matter how you scheme to get ahead, it will always come back to bite you. 3. Solomon didn't have a clue as to what Adonijah was doing until he was exposed. Solomon didn't say a word until he was put on the throne. What's for you is for you and only you. There were people fighting on Solomon's behalf and he was nowhere around.
4. It's not always HOW MANY are on your side, but WHO is on your side. If God be for you, who can be against you?
Play offense!

## WHY FAST?

Isaiah 58. In this chapter, Israel was seeking to know why they hadn't gotten the responses from God after they fasted. They asked the questions (verse 3),"Why have we fasted and you have not seen? Why have we humbled ourselves, and you have not noticed?"

WRONG FASTING: God replies, "On your day of fasting you do as you please and exploit all your workers. Your fasting ends in quarreling and strife, and in striking each other with wicked fists. YOU CANNOT FAST AS YOU DO TODAY AND EXPECT YOUR VOICE TO BE HEARD ON HIGH. Is this the kind of fast I have chosen, only a day for a man to humble himself? Is it only for bowing one's head like a reed and for lying on sackcloth and ashes? Is that what you call a fast, a day acceptable to the Lord?

TRUE FASTING: Is not this the kind of fast I have chosen: to loose the chains of injustice and untie the cords of the yoke, to set the oppressed free and break every yoke? Is it not to share your food with the hungry and to provide the poor wanderer with shelter when you see the naked, to clothe him, and not to turn away from you own flesh and blood?

RESULTS: Then your light will break forth like the dawn and your healing will quickly appear; then your righteousness will go before you, and the glory of the Lord will be your rear guard. Then you will call and the Lord will answer; you will cry for help and he will say: Here I am."

CONCLUSION: Is your fasting in vain?

## ONE MORE TIME

Luke chapter 5. In this chapter, Simon (the fisherman) and his co-workers had been fishing all night and hadn't caught anything. They figured that today wasn't their day so the began washing their nets out. Jesus jumped in his boat and told him to go out into the deep and let down their nets (verse

4). Simon replied, "Master, we've worked hard all night and haven't caught anything. But because you say so, I will let down the nets."

-REVELATION/UNDERSTANDING: It's not WHAT you're doing it's WHERE you're doing it. You may need to relocate.

NOTICE: You don't relocate without getting the directions. Jesus gave the directions. Is He giving the directions in your life?

**Simon washing the nets represented him giving up on his mission. In his mind, that day was not his day so he was quitting for the day.

**Life can deal us some blows and we may not get what we expected, but don't give up. Don't wash your nets. Even if you feel like you need a break, don't wash your nets permanently. Get the RIGHT instructions and cast it out there again.

Just because the last relationship didn't give you the results you wanted, cast your net somewhere else (and don't let the fear of not catching anything, stop you from throwing it out there). The sea is full of fish. You just need to get the RIGHT instructions.

-Yes there may be a shortage of "jobs", but David tells us in Psalm 37:25 "I was young but now am old, yet I've never seen the righteous forsaken or their children begging for bread."

CONCLUSION: God owns everything, even us. Throw your net out with the same expectations. Just make sure you throw it where He says throw it!

Love and Light

## SHIFT

I randomly opened up my Bible and I turned right to Isaiah 61. The first thing I saw was verse 2 which reads, "to proclaim the year of the Lord's favor and the day of vengeance of our God, to comfort all who mourn, (v3) and to provide for those who grieve in Zion-bestow on them a crown of beauty instead of ashes, the oil of gladness instead of mourning, and a garment of praise instead of a spirit of despair. They will be called oaks of righteousness, a planting of the Lord for the display of His splendor." -Many of you know but many of you may not know but Genarlow Wilson (the teenager who had consensual sex with another teenager) was set free on Friday October 26th.

GOD IS SHIFTING THINGS! You MUST read the entire chapter of Isaiah 61! Take 1 minute to read it and spend the rest of the day meditating on it. We have the tendency to allow our jobs to dictate much of our day and we set aside the information that is so simple but LIFE CHANGING! Read it and study it. Then watch the news tonight. Pay attention to how God is shifting things. Pay attention to the SHIFT.

## REFLECTOR

2 Samuel chapter 12. There is so much to learn from this chapter that you MUST read it for yourself. Sometimes we can get so comfortable in the day to day ritual of life that we don't take the time to reflect on the things that will keep us spiritually focused and grounded. We allow a few moments of being carefree to lead us into sinful situations. Getting control of the flesh will help navigate us into the right direction but the only way to do that is by following after the spirit man (Romans 8:5-9) We all need a "REFLECTOR"

--Nathan was the "REFLECTOR". He took time to remind David of all the things that God had did for him, unfortunately it was AFTER the sin. Take some time and go to the person or people you love and be their reflector and let's uplift one another BEFORE we sin.

## OUT OF PLACE

2 Samuel chapter 11. In this chapter, King David takes another man's wife, sleeps with her, and then orders the man whose wife he slept with to be put into an atmosphere to be killed.

This all could have been prevented had David been where he was supposed to be.

verse 1- In the spring at the time when kings go off to war, David sent Joab out with the king's men and the whole Israelite army. They destroyed the Amonites and besieged

Rabbi. ***But David remained in Jerusalem. (verse 2) One evening David got up from his bed and walked around on the roof of the palace. From the roof he saw a woman bathing.
The woman was very beautiful, and David sent someone to find out about her.
*REVELATION/UNDERSTANIDNG:* It is close to impossible to avoid things that will bring out our sinful nature. Our chances of escaping are a lot greater however; when we are where we are supposed to be, doing what we are supposed to be doing. When we are out of place, we open ourselves up and invite opportunities for sin to enter. David should've been at war with the rest of the kings, but he found himself out of place, which led him to be exposed to something he shouldn't have been.
--Be careful not to put yourself in a situation that will get you out of place. If you read the rest of the story, you will find that David sinned and compounded it and even tried to cover it up.
CLOSING REMARKS: A few good minutes (seconds for most of us) can get us into 20 years of trouble. Is a few good minutes worth it?

## HELP MIS-INTERPRETED

2 Samuel 10 verse 1- In the course of time, the king of the Ammonites died, and his son Hanun succeeded him as king. David thought, "I will show kindness to Hanun son of Nahash, just as his father showed kindness to me." So David sent a delegation to express his sympathy to Hanun concerning his father. When David's men came to the land of he Ammonites, the Ammonite nobles said to Hanun their Lord," Do you think David is honoring your father by sending men to you to

express sympathy? Hasn't David sent them to you to explore the city and spy it out and overthrow it?"
REVELATION/UNDERSTANDING:
There are times in our life when we intimidate people because of past victories. David was a warrior to heart but he was also a man of compassion. Even though he was going to show kindness to Hanun, the Nobles (ironic) in Hanun's camp couldn't recognize when someone was going to do good to them.
-Make sure you don't mis-interpret help. This is why it is IMPERATIVE to be in relationship with God for your self because He will reveal who to accept help from and who not to accept help from.
--Oftentimes people are quicker to side on the defensive rather than the offensive. But when you are living right (RIGHTEOUS), there is nothing to be defensive about. You will begin to EXPECT people to be a blessing to you!! It will become a way of life. Then when someone shows up with motives that are impure, you'll spot it almost immediately.
Proverbs 16:7 "When a man's ways please the Lord, He makes even his enemies to be at peace with him."
Be blessed!

## IT DOESN'T MATTER

2 Samuel chapter 3. (verse 1) Now there was long war between the house of Saul and the house of David: but David waxed (grew) stronger and stronger, and the house of Saul waxed weaker and weaker.
*REVELATION/UNDERSTANDING*: It doesn't matter what your enemies try to do, when God has His hand on you, it's on you!
-PROCESS- Please note that there still was a long battle!! Don't think that the enemy is just going to lay down and quit because you got anointed for an assignment. Embrace the

process!! Just because David was anointed to be the king, didn't mean that the road was going to be easy.

-God knows how to ware down your opposition and build you up at the same time. It doesn't matter who doesn't like it.

CONCLUSION: In verse 21, Abner decided that it was better to join David than to fight against him. Your enemies may never join you, but the writing will be on the wall that they can't defeat you. You just need to know it.

Have an "it doesn't matter" day.

## STOP PURSUING

2 Samuel chapter 2. In this chapter, a fight had broken out between a few of the tribes within the Children of Israel. Abner, (captain of Saul's host) lost a battle to David's men (verse 17)

-After Abner was defeated, he ran away and ended up being chased by a guy named Asahel. Abner asked him twice to stop following him but he would not listen.

(verse 23) Howbeit he refused to turn aside: wherefore Abner with the hinder end of the spear smote him under the fifth rib, that the spear came out behind him; and he fell down there, and died in the same place:

REVELATION/UNDERSTANDING: Be careful not to antagonize people when they are having a rough day. Why chase after someone if you aren't going to do anything?

-Following to close can get you killed. Let him/her who has ears hear.

## FIND SOMETHING GOOD

2 Samuel chapter 1.

OVERVIEW-Saul (who was the king) and his son Jonathan (who was next in line for the throne) died in the battle and David is about to be anointed.

-Verse 23- Saul and Jonathan were lovely and pleasant in their lives, and in their death they were not divided. They were swifter than eagles. They were stronger than lions. (24) Ye daughters of Israel, weep over Saul, who clothed you in scarlet, with other delights, who put on ornaments of gold upon your apparel.

UNDERSTANDING: Even though Saul tried to destroy and murder David, David found something good to say about Saul and Jonathan after the relationship was over.

-We sometimes wait for the relationship to be over to start venting about how bad a person was or how deserving they were for what they got. We tend to go negative before we go positive. We even question ourselves sometimes.

THERE IS NOTHING MORE WRONG WITH YOU THAN THERE IS WITH EVERYBODY ELSE. WE ALL HAVE ISSUES!!!!!

-The season had to end so that the next one can begin.

-Take the good from the person and relationship and spread it, because you never know who is talking good or bad about you. Remember, you get back what you put out!!

--David may have THOUGHT negative things he could've said about Saul, but we will never know because he kept them as just that, THOUGHTS!

CLOSING: Find the good and speak about it. ONLY GOOD! Closer than you think!

## A CHANCE – A TOUCHABLE – THE NERVE

I Samuel chapter 26. In this chapter, David is still on the run from King Saul, who has pursued after him into the mountains to kill him. There are a few things that we must pay attention to in this particular passage. (verse 5) Then David set out and went to the place where Saul had camped. He saw where Saul and Abner son of Ner, the commander of the army, had lain down. SAUL WAS LYING INSIDE THE CAMP, WITH THE ARMY ENCAMPED AROUND HIM.

-Saul and his men were sound asleep and David had A CHANCE to kill him, but instead, look what he says (verse 9) "Don't destroy him! Who can lay a hand on the Lord's anointed and be guiltless?"

--You might have A CHANCE to personally destroy your enemies, but let God fight your battles. It had to be difficult for David (who by the way, didn't ASK for any of this) to know that this man was trying to kill him, but still have mercy on him.

--You have some ammunition to destroy someone, but that's not the answer. Keep your hands clean!

QUOTE- "If you give your enemies enough rope, they'll hang themselves"

(Author unknown)

--SAUL WAS A TOUCHABLE- He was in the midst of the camp surrounded by his army, but David still got to him.

*REVELATION*: If God wants you to get to a person, you WILL get to them, no matter how high up they are.

PAY ATTENTION: The reason why God hasn't allowed YOU to get to that ndividual is because He knows what you will do when you get there! Who knows, maybe you'll forget about God!

-God knew what David was going to do once he got to Saul so He helped him. (verse 12) David took the spear and water jug by Saul's head, and they left. No one saw or knew about it, nor did anyone wake up. They were all sleeping, BECAUSE the LORD had put them into a deep sleep.

-THE NERVE-David had the nerve to go to Saul, even though he was running from him.

-Do you have the nerve to go and face your enemy? Do you have the nerve to go to the top? Do you have the nerve to go into the midst of the enemies' camp?

TIMING- Timing is everything! David was wise about when he went.

Closer than you think!

## DEEPER PART 1

I Samuel chapter 21 is leading me to one word. DEEPER!

--(verse 1) David went to Nob, to Ahimelech the priest. Ahimelech trembled when he met him, and asked, "Why are you alone? Why is no one with you?"

QUESTION: Have you ever been in a place where this question was applicable to you? Have you found yourself all alone?

-You can be with people who you known your whole life, but still be alone. You can be with a spouse for many years and be all alone. You can be with family, and still be all alone. You can even be with "church folk" and still be alone.

EXTREME MAKEOVER:

People that knew you to be one way, will look up and see someone totally different. They recognized David on the outside, but the real makeover was happening on the inside.

*REVELATION/UNDERSTANDING:* Just like David, God is calling us into a deeper relationship with Him.

-David did not ask for the anointing, that literally put him on the run. POINT- When God calls you in deeper, you become a lot more spiritual than religious. You do things that won't make sense to the average person. You talk differently, walk differently, and act differently.

--You MUST keep in your mind that God is pleased with obedience and therefore, you will need to be delivered from people and the OPINIONS of people.

-FACT- you will ask questions. You will ask questions you thought you'd never ask. Most of them will start with "WHY".

-Keep going - you are in a great place. It may not feel good, but it is necessary for where He is taking you.

CONCLUSION: 1. David lied to the priest about why he was on the run (verse 2-5). 2. David ate the "consecrated bread" (verse 6). 3. David took a weapon that he wasn't accustomed to using (Goliath's sword, verse 9). 4. David pretended to be a madman when he saw another king (verse 13).

SURVIVAL- David was doing what he needed to do to survive. Is this you?

Go DEEPER!

## DEATH

Many times in our lives we HATE to be corrected when we're wrong, especially when there's an audience on looking. Although we know everybody has been wrong at some point in their lives and have needed to be corrected, it still doesn't negate the fact that most of the time we feel embarrassed when corrected. The truth of the matter is that we ALL are going to die one day (some people don't like to talk about death but it is not only a REALITY, but death is also NECESSARY for those people around us.

In Mark chapter 8, Jesus is telling his disciples that he must die and everything that will happen to him up to his resurrection. Peter doesn't want to believe it so he pulls Jesus to the side and begins to rebuke him (verse 32).

Jesus said "Get behind me Satan, You do not have in mind the things of God, but the things of men."

REVELATION/UNDERSTANDING: There are some people in your life right now who you may not believe you can live without. There may be that one person who you don't know what you would do, if they were to pass on.

-Death is necessary people. In many cases, death lines up with purpose. We don't do the things we should oftentimes when we have people in our lives who will do them for us. We don't manage the money right until the person who always did it, passes on. We don't take care of our children until our caretaker moves on. We don't pay our own bills until the person who always provided for us, passes on or becomes a casualty in our lives.

-Jesus knew his purpose and although He wanted to stay around, He had to stay focused on his mission.

-Who do you need to rebuke? Who do you need to let know that you are leaving? Who do you need to give notice to that you are only in their life for a season?

-Some of you are dating a person right now who is in your life for a season-everybody is not permanent. Someone needs to put a child out of the house in 30 days. Some of you need to give your job their "2 weeks notice"

Death is necessary, but UNDERSTANDING and ACCEPTING that death is necessary is PRICELESS and WISDOM. Whether we want to face it or not! Enjoy the person/situation for the time you are appointed, but look ahead.

## DESPITE FEAR

In Ezra chapter 3 and verse 3 jumped out at me. Lately I have been getting emails and talking to people who are fearful in some capacity or another. A good friend of mine called me Wednesday night and said that he was fearful of his life because the attack from Satan was so intense in this particular season of his life.

Verse 3- "Despite their fear of the peoples around them, they built the altar on its foundation and sacrificed burnt offerings on it to the Lord, both the morning and evening sacrifices."

REVELATION/UNDERSTANDING: There are some situations in your life that will or have arrived that mean enough to you to make you move forward (even if you are still fearful). The only thing you have to decide is how much it/they/he/she means to you.

-Some of us are afraid to love. Some of us are afraid to start the new business. Some of us are afraid to trust. Some of us are afraid to make that purchase. Some of us are afraid to fly.

-Right around the September 11 attacks, my pastor talked about having to overcome his fear of flying in order to fulfill his obligations to people that booked him to speak.

-Despite his fear, his word meant enough to him to get on the plane so that he could fulfill the obligations.

The Israelites were still fearful but they felt like it was worth the risk to sacrifice to God who had delivered them. The fear was not removed, but God meant enough to them to move forward in this form of worship.

QUESTION: WHAT ARE YOU FEARFUL OF? AND WHAT IS STANDING ON THE OTHER SIDE OF THE FEAR? COULD IT BE THE BIGGEST BLESSING OF YOUR LIFE?

CONCLUSION: If there is ever a time to move forward (especially in the face of fear) it is to do something for God.

## NEWNESS

Today I would like to share a conversation that I had with a friend of mine last night. He and his wife of two years had been going through very rough times. They just couldn't seem to get on one accord about the money. They had lived in apartments, and even hotels. Then finally they bought a house. He has owned a good number of houses (8-10) and is in his mid 30's. She's in her late 30's and has never owned a house. His words to me last night were, "ever since we moved into the new house, I can honestly say that it's been PEACEFUL."

REVELATION/UNDERSTANDING: Although MATERIAL doesn't necessarily BUY happiness, it does have it's place. Newness in many occasions brings about excitement. Newness gives you something to look forward to. Newness sometimes makes you communicate in ways you haven't done (or haven't done in quite some time) and is beneficial to both of you. Picture this: (and remember it's the little things) This couple now has to pick out furniture together, decide on what colors they want in terms of paint, decide on what appliances they want.

-The bottom line is the fact that some of us just need some newness in our lives. New relationships, new surroundings, new cities, new automobiles, new jobs, new outlooks, new eating habits. NEW (This is not the time to be irresponsible and go crazy with your finances, but NEWNESS within your means is a good thing.

CONCLUSION: My mother has slept in the same bed for thirty-something years and recently got a new bed. Her excitement and vibrancy just from getting a new bed is remarkable. Imagine when she moves out of the same house she's been in for the same amount of time.

## FAMILY

Mark chapter 6.

QUESTION: Have you ever gone off to college, the military, prison or spent significant time away from the place and people you grew up with? Were you the type of person that nobody expected to be anything extraordinary? In this chapter, Jesus returned to his hometown (Nazareth) with his disciples and look what the people who he grew up with had to say. (Verse 2) "Where did this man get these things?" they asked. "What 's this wisdom that has been given him, that he even does miracles! (verse 3) "ISN'T THIS THE CARPENTER? ISN'T THIS MARY'S SON AND THE BROTHER OF JAMES, JOSEPH, JUDAS AND SIMON? AREN'T HIS SISTERS HERE WITH US?"

REVELATION/UNDERSTANDING-Your ending will be better than your beginning. It is not to late to do what God has called you to. It might require you to go away for a while. Don't get caught up in who you leave behind, after all, somebody needs to be a witness. Somebody has to know what you used to do and who you used to be because once they see that you've changed then they'll believe that they can change.

-PARENTS- It's not so bad to make your kids work instead of giving them everything. It's not so bad to make them mow lawns, shovel snow, work on cars, clean houses. We sometimes get into trouble because we don't know how to let go. You have to let go sometimes in order to give life.

-Jesus left home as a boy and came back as a miracle worker. CONCLUSION: Don't hold folk back because you didn't have the nerve to step out when purpose was calling you. Those who are going to step out, just know that your FAITH in God will be honored and once you return, people who knew you back when will see things in you that will be astonishing.

-It's like a child growing up- When you see them everyday, it's difficult to see them sprouting, but when you haven't seen them in a while, it's amazing to you how they've stretched out.

-The people will see it, and some will be amazed-but YOU gotta do it.

## HOW ARE YOU PLANTED

Mark chapter 4. In this chapter, Jesus explains four types of seeds. 1. Seeds that fell on the path (they weren't planted so the birds came and ate them). 2. Seeds that fell on rocky places with a little soil (they weren't deep enough so they grew up but quickly withered because the root wasn't deep enough). 3. Seeds that fell among thorns (that grew up but got choked by the cares of this world). 4. Seeds that fell on good soil (that produced fruit). REVELATION/UNDERSTANDING: We must have a good teacher inspired/chosen by God who will properly sow/plant the Word into our lives. It is not totally up to us to teach ourselves, but we do have our part to play by attending services or connection groups that will properly sow/plant the Word.

-Some of us don't care to be planted because we are to busy doing our own thing. We sometimes think that just "going" to church is enough.

PARABLE: Church is like a hospital. A hospital tends to the needs of the sick. It is supposed to be a place where people can go to get well. If a sick person went to a hospital and sat in a room and was never tended to, the hospital itself would only be a building or structure to that individual just like a bank with no money would be to a person who is going in to get money out. What type of treatment are you getting for your sickness? What are you taking to make you well so that you won't re-visit the same sickness? What are you cutting out of your daily diet that will keep you out of the hospital? How deep are you planted?

## BREAK OUT

Mark chapter 1. It's amazing how God will prepare us for His purpose and plan but it's equally amazing how we often fail to listen or line-up with what He says. Yesterday we talked about disconnecting and look where He has us today. (Verse 16) As Jesus walked beside the Sea of Galilee, he saw Simon and his brother Andrew casting a net into the lake, for they were fishermen. (Verse 17) "Come, follow me, " Jesus said, "and I will Make you fishers of men." (Verse 18) At once they left their nets and followed him. (Verse 19) When he had gone a little further, He saw James son of Zebedee and his brother John in a boat, preparing their nets. (Verse 20) Without delay he called them, and they left their father Zebedee in the boat with the hired men and followed Him.

REVELATION/UNDERSTANDING: When God calls us, we have to "break out". We sometimes have apprehension for a plethora of reasons. 1. We don't know where we're going. 2. We only know where we've been and aren't used to living OUTSIDE of our comfort zone. 3. We are afraid to leave family and friends behind. 4. We are afraid to disconnect from our support (job, boyfriend/girlfriend, city, or even the school we attend) in order to live our purpose.

-EQUIPPED- Don't you understand that you have already been equipped with the tools necessary to follow Jesus? In this particular situation, the men Jesus called were fishermen. They didn't become fishermen after they met Jesus. They already had the skills. The only thing Jesus was going to show them was how to re-direct their skill from what they did (catch fish) to catch men. Yes the bait may be different, but the skill is already there.

-You have skills as well and God wants to use you and those skills to help build the kingdom.

-Notice how they all left immediately. None of us lived back in those days but I think it's fair to say that they didn't have the distractions that we now have. It was clear to them (for whatever reason) that their whole life up to this point was preparation for living their purpose. They left family, jobs, security and what they knew to be home, in order to live their purpose.

-I think it's also fair to say that none of them knew what to expect, they just left when they were called.

-What is God telling you to do today? HOW long will you continue to sit in your cubicle miserable equipped with skills that aren't being utilized? How long will you endure the misery of complacency? How long will you continue to question the outcome of your life?

-You will NEVER be fulfilled, be peaceful or joyful until you do what God wants you to do. Today is your day to BREAK OUT and nobody can BREAK OUT for you so quit waiting for them to fire you. Quit waiting for them to kick you out. Quit waiting to get evicted. Quit waiting for them to dump you. Quit waiting for them to ordain you. Quit waiting for your money to be right (it ain't gon' ever be right). BREAK OUT!

## DIS-CONNECT

Ezekiel chapter 31. verse 16 "I made the nations tremble at the sound of its fall when I brought it down to the grave with those who go down to the pit. Then all the trees of Eden, the choicest and best of Lebanon, all the trees that were well watered, were consoled in the earth below. (verse 17) Those who lived in its shade, its ALLIES among the nations, had ALSO gone down to the grave with it, joining those killed by the sword."

REVELATION/UNDERSTANDING: There are some people that have linked up with people (leaders, pastors, politicians, city officials, co-workers, bosses) that have been proud and haughty. They are going to spin, crash and burn and you will also if you don't disconnect. Disconnect, or surely you WILL go down with them.

-You and your household will come to want. The abundance you once knew will be restrained. The people who befriended you because of your status will fade away. It will be a lonely time for you and yours.

## WHAT ARE YOU DOING WITH IT?

Matthew chapter 25. In this chapter, Jesus gave the parable about the master who gave three of his servants different amounts of money (TALENTS) to see what they would do with them while he went away on business (verse 15). The first he gave 5 talents. The second he gave 2 talents. The third he gave 1 talent.

-The one he gave five talents to, gained another five. The one he gave two, gained another two, but the one he gave a single talent to, buried his and had nothing to give back to the master except what was given to him.

REVELATION/UNDERSTANDING: How many talents has God given to you and what are you doing with it/them? God did not give you gifts and talents to bury in the ground.

-It's amazing how we will sit on a job, MISERABLE, when we have gifts inside of us that will bring us both joy and money. We get CAUGHT up permanently, in a situation that was meant to be temporary.

***I'm not talking about God having us in a particular season, because there are exceptions (like being humbled)****

What are you doing with your TALENT(S)/Gift(s)? Is it an issue of trust or fear that you haven't moved? I know that there are some of you who LOVE to sing (and God has given you songs, but you are afraid, slothful or distrustful). Some of you are great artists, writers, dancers, preachers, but because it requires an act of faith, trust and living out of the box, and being validated by your loved ones, you won't move. Somebody branded in our heads that although we have these gifts, they won't pay the bills for us. (Maybe it's time to downgrade so that we can do what we love to do). Maybe its time to get rid of unnecessary things like (cable, extra phone lines, charge cards, ring tones and other unnecessary things that put a strain on our pockets and minds, so that we can move in our gifts/talents and afford to live and be happy.

-Some of us are just plain LAZY. We want the money, fame, and luxury of firing our current bosses but we don't want to do what it takes to get there. You CANNOT shortcut the process.

PROVERBS 18:16 "Your Gifts will make room for you, and bring you into the presence of the great."

-Sometimes we just have to work our talents/gifts. 2 Timothy 1:6 "For this reason I remind you to fan into flame the gift of God" (verse 7) "For God did not give us a spirit of timidity (fear), but a spirit of power, of love and of self-discipline.

****Some of us have been sold that our EDUCATION will do it. Not So! It may enhance the gift, but it alone doesn't make room for you to move into God's plan for your life.

(EXAMPLE) You can't teach flawless beauty- that comes from God. You can't teach a voice like Aretha Franklin - that comes from God. You can't teach a photographic memory - that comes from God.

CONCLUSION: I challenge you to write down YOUR gifts/talents. If you don't know what it/they are, ask God. You CAN'T pay attention to what society says about your talent no matter how big or little it may be. Remember- God ordains relationships, Not man. God will take something small and put you with someone great.

TESTIMONY: I have a friend who went to college to be an accountant. She like numbers but knew she had more inside of her. She worked with me on my first movie (never did anything pertaining to movies in her life, but loved it. She had the talent of organization and pulling things together. Seven years later, this accountant who knew God had more for her, now works as the personal assistant for the biggest name in filmmaking. She stirred her gift/talent, and left a "good" paying job to do so.

What are you doing with your talent?

## INVITATION

Matthew chapter 22. Jesus opens by giving a parable about the kingdom of heaven. verse 2- "The kingdom of heaven is like a king who prepared a wedding banquet for his son. He sent his servants to those who had been invited to the banquet to tell them to come, but they refused to come. (Verse 4) Then he sent some more servants and said, 'Tell those who have been invited that I have prepared my dinner: My oxen and fattened cattle have been butchered, and everything is ready. Come to the wedding banquet.' Question: Have YOU accepted God's invitation?

REVELATION/UNDERSTANDING: We sometimes don't accept God's invitation because of who is giving the party. We feel like the party will be boring or filled with lifeless people. We feel like we can't do the things we have become accustomed to doing at other parties. A party in our eyes is different than a party in His eyes. We want to continue to do our own thing that gratifies the flesh (not knowing that we can still gratify the flesh [even though the rules may be different]). Sometimes we won't accept the invitation because of what our "friends" will think.  verse 5 But they paid no attention and went off- one to his field, another to his business.

Conclusion: God went through the trouble of preparing the party for us, the least we can do is reply. Bottom-line: Some of us want Jesus and some of us Don't! Which do you choose? I've never asked any of you who receive the devotions to forward them, but today I am asking for you to forward this to people in your database who you KNOW aren't Saved. Out of those people, I am asking that you pick one and treat them to a meal. At the meal, open your heart and allow God to use you. (Without being super holy or religious). A good ice-breaker may be to share something personal about yourself (just a suggestion).

**useFUL or useLESS**

Matthew chapter 21 verse 43, "Therefore I tell you that the kingdom of God will be taken away from you and given to a people who will produce its fruit. (verse 44) he who falls on this stone will be broken, but he on whom it falls will grind him to powder."

QUESTION: Are YOU doing what YOU can to produce fruit for the kingdom? Some of us have been in church for years and haven't even invited someone to attend with us, let alone share the Word of God with them (myself included)!

BROKEN vs CRUSHED: When I allow Christ to be the Lord of my life, I have agreed (sometimes subconsciously) to be broken, because the Word (which is Jesus) will break us from doing what we totally want to doing what He wants. Would you rather be broken but useful to God or be ground to powder and useless?

CHARACTER- Lord, please break me so that I may be used by you to bring fruit into the kingdom.

Please read whole chapter.

## TAX TIME

Matthew chapter 17 verse 25- 27 "What do you think Simon, he asked. "From whom do the kings of the earth collect duty and taxes-from their own sons or from others?" (26) "From others", Peter answered. "Then the sons are exempt," Jesus said to him. "But so that we may not offend them, go to the lake and throw out your line. Take the first fish you catch; open its mouth and you will find a four-drachma coin. Take it and give it to them for my tax and yours."

-Notice how Jesus sent Peter back to what he used to do (fishing) for a living to pay "their" tax. But also notice how Jesus PROVIDED the tax money.

-Peter did the work-Jesus provided the money.

REVELATION/UNDERSTANDING: Even though we may work for the Lord in some capacity, we still may be required to go and do what we used to do in order to handle our responsibilities. It didn't take Peter fifteen fish to pay off the duty. He did it on the first catch MIRACULOUSLY. Although you may be required to work, you won't have to work AS HARD. God provides quantitatively more for those who work for Him. If you take care of His business, He will take care of yours.

--When you work for God, you will miraculously receive bonuses, unexpected money, and other blessings that were not anticipated. And it will come when you need it the most.

## BRING'EM OUT BRING'EM OUT

I studied the 11th chapter of 2 Kings. In this chapter, a woman named Athaliah went forth to kill the royal family because her son Ahaziah was killed (verse 1). (verse 2) But Jehosheba, the daughter of King Jehoram and sister of Ahaziah, took Joash son of Ahaziah and stole him away from among the royal princes, who were about to be murdered. She put him and his nurse in a bedroom to hide him from Athaliah; so he was not killed. He remained hidden with his nurse at the temple of the Lord for six years while Athaliah ruled the land.

REVELATION/UNDERSTANDING: God has been preserving some of us in the temple but He's about to make us billboards. You thought your life was over and thought that God forgot about you. You thought that your spiritual education was going to go to waste. You thought that your life didn't have meaning, and so did the bystanders.

-The bystanders have been socializing with a giant and didn't notice it. The bystanders couldn't recognize God's anointed because it wasn't your time yet. The process wasn't complete yet.

--Joash began to reign at 7 years old-- but he didn't choose himself, God chose him. Why? Because God made a covenant with David that the Messiah would flow through his descendants (2 Samuel 7). There is no way to do that if everybody is dead.

--SAFETY--The priest (Jehoida) ordered for the commanders of units of hundreds to protect the king. They surrounded him (verse4-7) VERSE 8-"Station yourselves around the king, each man with his weapon in his hand. Anyone who approaches your ranks, MUST be put to death. Stay close to the king wherever he goes."

-The people that would've destroyed you - forgot about you. The people that wrote you off are in for a tremendous surprise.

-CONCLUSION-The time has come for you to be revealed. God has not and cannot lie. Every word He has spoken will come to pass.

--If this isn't you, pay attention to the people that God raises up and reveals. The best thing you can do is support them and be a blessing to them.

**WHEN YOU MAKE UP YOUR MIND**

2Kings chapter 7. This is the story of the four leprous men who sat at the entrance of the city gate of Samaria where there was a famine/siege taking place. They said to one another (verse 4),"Why stay here until we die? If we say, 'We'll go into the city' -the famine is there, and we will die. And if we stay here, we will die. So let's go over to the camp of the Arameans and surrender. If they spare us, we live; if they kill us, then we die."

REVELATION/UNDERSTANDING: some of you are in a position like the 4 leprous men. Either way you turn, you have nothing to lose. Where you are right now is stagnant and fruitless, and where you came from is stagnant and fruitless.

--The answer for you is quite simple, fall into the hands of the Living God and walk into territory you know nothing about.

--It's important to note that the four leprous men made up their mind at DUSK (verse 5), because as soon as they made up their minds at DUSK, God had already made provision for them in the territory they were seeking to go to (see verse 7).

--Once you make up your mind that you are not going to die in the middle of this mess, God will lead you to where you need to go.

--QUIT COMPLAINING IF YOUR NOT GOING TO DO SOMETHING ABOUT IT. QUIT TRYING TO MAKE PEOPLE FEEL SORRY FOR YOU AND DO SOMETHING ABOUT YOUR SITUATION T-O-D-A-Y!

## WHEN YOU MAKE UP YOUR MIND – PART 2

2Kings chapter 7, piggybacking off of yesterdays word. RECAP: Thee was a sore famine in the land of Samaria. There were four leprous men who sat at the gate of the city who weighed their options (verse 4) "if we go into the city, then the famine is there and we shall die. If we stay here doing nothing, we will die also." The four leprous men had the option of complaining OR being proactive to change their situation. They chose to CHANGE their situation. In doing so, look what happened - (Verse 8) The men who had leprosy reached the edge of the camp and entered one of the tents. They ate, drank, and carried away silver, gold and clothes and went off and HID them. They returned and entered another tent and took some things from it and HID them also. (verse 9) Then they said to each other, "We're not doing right. This is a day of good news and we are keeping it to ourselves. If we wait until daylight, punishment will overtake us. Let's go at once and report this to the royal palace."

REVELATION/UNDERSTANDING: In the midst of a famine/drought, if God gives you an abundance. SHARE. Greed has been one of the things that has kept some of us from growing closer to God and being even more blessed.

We sometimes think that by hoarding it all to ourselves, that we have a leg up on everybody else, or (subconsciously) attempt to make others feel like we are more blessed than them. Share! share! share! --Who knows when a drought/famine will come upon your household? When you give cheerfully with an open heart, God will see to it that in the midst of your famine, that someone will come and share THEIR abundance with you.

## SURVIVE

2Kings chapter 6. QUESTION: Can you imagine a famine or drought so severe that it causes people to eat their children?

This was the case in Samaria (see verses 25-29).

REVELATION/UNDERSTANDING: You find out who people really are when things seem to be at their worst. People did what they felt they had to do to survive. Kanye West has a verse in one of his songs that says, "to me, giving up is way harder than trying". As crazy as it may seem, the mother's who agreed to give up their sons for a meal did what they felt needed to be done to survive.

-Never say what you will or won't do in a particular situation until your in that situation. Don't judge others for doing what they feel needs to be done to survive. Only God can judge us!

UNDERSTAND: Look at the reason why there is a famine or drought in the first place. (verse 24) "Some time later, Ben-Hadad king of Aram mobilized his entire army and marched up and laid siege to Samaria. (25) There was a great famine in the city; the siege lasted so long that a donkey's head sold for eighty shekels of silver and a quarter of a cab of seed pods for five shekels.

--The famine came at the hands of a man and his army.

--For those of you who are in a famine/drought because of a person or group of people, do what you have to do to SURVIVE. God allowed them to do it **FOR A SEASON** you do what you have to do to survive (within His boundaries)

--You might be going through the roughest time of your life, but stay alive!

I talked to two different individual since Sunday and the first one stated," I am ready for '07' to be over and am ready for '08'" She said it with such desperation and urgency, like all of her effort and energy had been spent. Then the other young lady said with such peace and calmness, "I know that you may disagree, but I think I am going to leave my husband. I can't go into '08' like this, unhappy and struggling."

--REVELATION/UNDERSTANDING: Does it do us any good to be in the season of spring if the conditions are still that of the winter? In other words, we know when the calendar says the first official day of spring starts, but God will keep snow on the ground and cold air all around us until He has finished killing/freezing off old stuff so that new stuff can live.

--Embrace the season your in. Be spiritual enough to look past the famine or drought and consult God about the bigger picture.

--This is not the time to quit, this is the time to SURVIVE.

## YOU START IT

I Kings chapter 20. In this chapter, God sent a prophet to Ahab (king of Israel) to let him know that he was sending him to battle against his enemy (Ben-Hadad). Notice the conversation. (Verse 13) Meanwhile a prophet came to Ahab king of Israel and announced, "This is what the Lord says: 'Do you see this vast army? I will give it into you hand today, and then you will know that I am the Lord.'" "But who will do this?" asked Ahab. The prophet replied, "This is what the Lord says: 'The young officers of the provincial commanders will do it.'" "And who will start the battle?" he asked. The prophet answered, "You will."

REVELATION/UNDERSTANDING: You are not considered a bully if you start a fight ordained by God. Quit waiting for the enemy to attack you-you attack the enemy. Are you waiting for the boss to give you a well-deserved raise or are you going to go in and DEMAND one? Are you going to wait for the bank to take your house, or are you going to go to the bank and DEMAND a better loan? Are you going to wait for your girlfriend/boyfriend to put you out because you don't want to live in sin anymore, or are you going to make the first MOVE? YOU START IT! GOD HAS FINISHED IT!!!!!

## WEARY

Have you ever grown weary trying to do the things of God? Have you ever had moments when you felt like you'd rather just Die than to try to live a life of righteousness? Have you ever been in a place where even though you KNOW you've been obedient, and God didn't move like you thought HE would, it made you question if He was still going to be faithful to you and "your promises"?

--When God says in Matthew 20:16 that "Many are Called but few are Chosen," He means that you can't quit. Something inside of you won't allow you to quit.

Example: When you were younger and would be outside with your friends, your parents or guardians would CALL you in from playing. Most of the time you'd respond by going in the house-but there were times when you'd act like you didn't hear them. LOL. You had a choice that day of whether you'd answer the call or ignore it. When you are CHOSEN- you actually have NO choice but to go because you've been hand selected. I Kings chapter 19. Please read the chapter--This was Elijah's season to feel like he was ready to give up. Just at the breaking point, God came in and gave him food and rest so that he could continue his journey. Elijah felt like he was the only one doing God's will. He also felt like He had put his life on the line by being obedient, but I (Jay) say that we put our lives on the line when we are NOT obedient. God knows our weary times. Be in a place with Him where you can detect His STILL SMALL VOICE.

## THE BANK

I Kings chapter 16. This whole chapter was dedicated to 5 different Kings of Israel (each reigning one after another) who committed sin against God and caused the people of Israel to commit sin.

THE BANK- Yesterday evening, me and anther gentleman went to the bank to conduct some business. We went to a banking branch inside of a grocery store that was located in the heart of the West End. Demographically, it is considered to be lower economical as far as wealth is concerned. The gentleman lives a few blocks from the bank and told me that every time he comes into this particular grocery store (not only to bank but also to shop) that there are always long lines and long waiting periods.

EXAMPLE: There was a family in front of us and there were two young girls within that family ranging in age from 10-13. I expressed to the gentleman that even though I don't and won't sentence those young girls to everlasting sameness, as long as they see and experience these long waiting periods and lines out the door, the more susceptible they are to accepting this type of service (THINKING THAT THIS IS THE WAY ITS SUPPOSED TO BE).

*REVELATION/UNDERSTANDING*: Just like the kings in this chapter that followed the examples of those who came before them, so will the people who are looking at you.

QUESTION: Although none of us are perfect, are you doing everything in your power to live a life that is not only pleasing to God, but one that will not cause the people around you to sin? Let's make up in our minds that we are going to break the curses and walk the talk!

**IT TAKES NERVE**

I Kings Chapter 15. In this chapter, Asa (King of Judah) had to make a decision to either make God happy or make his relatives and community happy. Asa did what he could to eliminate the things that displeased God while he was on the throne, including demoting his grandmother from "Queen Mother", because she made an idol (verse 11-13).

*REVELATION/UNDERSTANDING:* There are times in our lives where we will have the opportunity to choose what will be pleasing to God as opposed to pleasing the people around us. It takes Nerve to go against your mother, father and grandparents but will you do it if it means pleasing God? It takes Nerve to leave your surroundings after generations have been there. It takes Nerve to rebel against what friends consider to be cool when you know God is displeased.

Do you have the Nerve it takes to be different? 1 KINGS 14

When wealth, idol worship and immorality become more important than God, everything will take a short time to dissipate. When God is gone from our lives, everything else becomes useless, no matter how valuable it seems.

You must read I Kings chapter 14.

## U O BAY

I Kings chapter 13 which persuades me to start off with a question. How many times have you been told by God exactly what or whatnot to do and disobeyed? verse 9- "For I was commanded by the word of the Lord: 'You must not eat bread or drink water or return by the way you came.'"

(Verse 15) So the prophet said to him," Come home with me and eat." (16) The man of God said, "I cannot turn back and go with you, nor can I eat bread or drink water with you in this place. I have been told by the word of the Lord: 'You must not eat bread or drink water there or return by the way you came.'" verse 18- The old prophet answered," I too am a prophet, as you are. And an angel said to me by the word of the Lord: 'Bring him back with you to your house so that he may eat bread and drink water.'" (But he was lying to him.) So the man of God returned with him and ate and drank in his house.

*REVELATION/UNDERSTANDING:* When God tells YOU to do something, DO IT! Quit waiting for people to validate what you were told to do.

--When you hear from God, you don't have to explain the instructions to people. If He tells you to walk away from a job or person or situation, BE OUT!

--Somebody needs to tell their boss TODAY!, I'm Out! Not at my words, but at God's words.

CHURCH FOLK-No matter how bad we may want people to believe we're anointed, quit propheLYING to people trying to make them believe that you have this one on one with God and only YOU can receive a word.

--If God told YOU that he/she is your spouse, don't you think He revealed that to them? BOTTOM LINE- U O BAY, and don't let people get you off track or doing contrary to what God told YOU to do! I hope this is the best day of your life!

## TURN OF EVENTS

I Kings chapter 12. Recap- King Solomon died and his son Rehoboam was next in line to succeed his father as the king. Right before he was made king by the people they came to him with a request to lighten the work load that King Solomon had put on them (verse 4). Rehoboam sent them away for three days until he could make a decision. In those three days Rehoboam consulted with the elders about what move he should make (verse 6-9). He didn't like what the elders had to say so he listened to the advice of his peers (people he grew up with).

*REVELATION:* If you are going to seek advice about a major decision, it's okay to ask friends and family; however, don't forget to consult the elders or people who have lived longer than you have.

--The people who you grew up with may be wise, but those who have live longer have seen more.

--The elders gave Rehoboam the answer that would give him control of the kingdom and create faithful servants, but not even the words of the elders can stop God from doing what He said He would do?

VERSE 15: So the king did not listen to the people, for this turn of events was from the Lord, to fulfill the word the Lord had spoken to Jeroboam son of Nebat through Ahijah the Shilonite (Chapter 11:29-39).

CONCLUSION: Whenever we sin against God, we put ourselves in a position to cause a TURN OF EVENTS. The answers that Rehoboam needed were given to him face to face, but God moved within to harden Jeroboam's heart against sound wisdom. Once we realize that God controls us and our enemies we have the opportunity to make better servants. -Don't do something to cause a sudden change of events in your life.

PRAYER: Lord, please take whatever sin that is in me, out of me so that I will not sin against you. Whatever you have to do to correct my ways, do so; but please don't take your spirit from me or allow me to get myself into trouble with you that will cause a sudden change in my destiny. In the name of Jesus I give thanks, and ask it all. AMEN!

## FINDING YOUR PURPOSE

As I study Matthew chapter 16, I wonder how many people still don't know their purpose for being here (on earth). verse 24- Then Jesus said to his disciples, "If anyone would come after me, he must deny himself and take up his cross and follow me. (Verse 25) For whoever wants to save his life will lose it, but whoever loses his life for me will find it. What good will it be for a man if he gains the whole world, and forfeits his own soul? Or what can a man give in exchange for his soul?

REVELATION/UNDERSTANDING: Many of us are miserable because we are in situations that have nothing to do with our purpose. We are not LIVING - We're EXISTING! We take abuse on the job because we are afraid to lose our job. We take abuse in relationships because we are afraid of being alone. We take abuse from our children because we're afraid to be parents. We go to bed harboring deep secrets that cause unrest, which results in having health issues. Jesus was telling his disciples that they cannot be concerned with the things that pertain to this world and follow him at the same time.

-"DENY HIMSELF"- When was the last time you denied yourself of something you strongly desired (outside of fasting)?

-"TAKE UP HIS CROSS"- Have you accepted Jesus as YOUR Lord & Savior? Many times we want Jesus to be our Savior so that we can have our sins forgiven and so we can get into Heaven but we seldom want Him to be our LORD.

Lord means Greek term 'Kurios' and it literally means CONTROLLER.

-If we let Jesus be our controller, then we will find our LIFE, but if we don't allow Him to be our controller, we are trying to save our own lives which in turn will cause us to lose it (or stay in situations that cause us to EXIST rather than LIVE).

CONCLUSION: Until we allow Jesus to be the CONTROLLER of our lives, we are just like the computers, tables, chairs, sofas, appliances, cubicles and lamps that sit in the dark when we cut the lights off. EXISTING rather than LIVING. Those things don't have life and vigor, but they are lifeless and only good to be USED by others.

**WHAT WOULD THEY SAY**

Ruth chapter 2. This is the story of one exceptional woman who did the unusual as it pertains to family and in-laws. The one thing that stuck out to me was her reputation. Your reputation is formed by the people who watch you at work in your community, in your home and where you worship. (Verse 7) She said, "'Please let me glean and gather among the sheaves behind the harvesters.' She went into the field and has worked steadily from morning till now, except for a short rest in the shelter."

GLEAN-means to pick up anything that is dropped or left over.

REVELATION/UNDERSTANDING: This past weekend, I went to a funeral in Cincinnati. The woman who passed was a mother of nine and had been married 50 years. She was a doer and not a talker. She was humble yet bold in that she picked up the leftovers (souls) on HER field.

-When it comes to funerals or sad occasions, we tend to read stats or play host to those people who take the stage and make up lies about the deceased because we feel like we have to say something positive. It doesn't matter if it was made up or not we just do it as people. However, we may find some differences in the statements made about the person.

-Ruth stuck out and as a result, she was given the king's protection (verse 8-9). It didn't matter who didn't like it whether it was the other gleaners, harvesters or overseers. She had the reputation for working hard and being humble to the point that the word spread quickly. She found favor and increased.

At The Funeral:

--Everybody said the same things about the deceased which I interpret as "everybody can't be lying!" When the majority can speak positive on behalf of your character, is it fair to say that this validates your reputation? What do the people in your home, sanctuary and community have to say about you? If you were to die today, who would come to your funeral and what would they say? What do you need to work on? What would make you a more pleasant person? What makes people not want to be around you? What is your service to society? What would they say?

## RESOLUTIONS

2 Corinthians chapter 7. Look at verse 1 "Since we have these promises, dear friends, let us purify ourselves from

everything that contaminates the body and spirit, perfecting holiness out of reverence for God."

-Right around the time we begin a new year, many of us have make resolutions. For some of us it's to lose weight, get out of debt, go to church, eat better, get married, get a new job etc.....

-REVELATION/UNDERSTANDING: If we will purify ourselves from everything that contaminates the body and spirit, the "resolutions" will take care of themselves. Whether it be people, food, television, internet, jobs etc whatever we purify ourselves from in an effort to reverence God, our resolutions will become a reality. MOTIVES- We sometimes fall short of completing our resolutions because of our motives. Not that our motives aren't good, but maybe they don't mean enough to us to stick to them. I propose that if our motives are to please God and grow closer to Him, it gives the fight/struggle more meaning.

EXAMPLE: Rather than trying to lose weight so that I can fit into an outfit, I choose to eat better because I am going to need my health to run the race that God has set before me. I am going to need to be in shape if I am going to travel all over the world to speak to people, I am going to need my health to be able to play with my children, I am going to need my health to keep from getting sick, I am going to eat better because I need to stay awake longer so that I can complete the tasks at hand rather than go to sleep after a meal etc... This is just an example, but there are many ways we can rid ourselves of things that contaminate our bodies and spirits.

-There will be effort involved, but making up our minds to REVERENCE God, makes the goal a bit easier to swallow.

## STILL SOME FIGHT LEFT IN YOU

2 Kings chapters 20-21. In 20, Hezekiah, (king of Judah) had an illness and was at the point of death. He received a word

from the prophet Isaiah stating that he was going to die so he should get his house in order (verse 1). Hezekiah turned his face to the wall and prayed to the Lord, "Remember, O Lord, how I have walked before you faithfully and with wholehearted devotion and have done what is good in your eyes." And Hezekiah wept bitterly.

QUESTION: Have you ever felt or thought to yourself "I can't die like this? Or there's got to be more! or I can't leave my kids like this!" Sometimes our conditions look so grim that we have capitulated to our current circumstances because the fight is just to taxing. We ourselves don't see a way out and our muscles aren't strong enough to withstand the weight. We haven't lived out our full potential but at the same time we haven't put forth the effort we know we could've because we were either afraid due to past failures or we allowed life (and other people) to determine our paths.

REVELATION/UNDERSTANDING- There is still some fight left in you. You do not have to die in the state you're in. You have one more praise payment. You have one more worship payment. You have one more prayer payment. God will give you the strength to get up and LIVE. You will not die like this. There is some fight still left in you. Refocus-Re-commit-Revive-Repent-Renew-Resolve and my dear friends REJOICE. If you are still weeping, God is not finished yet.

-Hezekiah wept bitterly because although he was sick, he felt like there was more for him to do. He still had some fight left and so do you.

VERSE 4- Before Isaiah had left the middle court, the word of the Lord came to him: "Go back and tell Hezekiah, the leader of my people, 'This is what the Lord, the God of your father David, says: I have heard you prayer and seen your tears; I will heal you. (verse 6) I will add fifteen years to your life. And I will deliver you and this city from the hand of the king of Assyria. I will defend this city for my sake and for the sake of my servant David.' "It's not over for you-THERE IS STILL SOME FIGHT LEFT IN YOU. What are you going to do with it?

## INTIMIDATED

2 Kings chapter 19. In this chapter, King of Assyria (Sennacherib) continued to threaten and attempt to intimidate Hezekiah (king of Judah). Sennacherib tried to intimidate Hezekiah by using the facts of the past (vs. 10-13).

-MISTAKES- Although Sennacherib stated facts, he stated facts about defeating people who didn't believe in the LIVING God.

\*\*\*It doesn't matter what your past losses consisted of BEFORE you walked with God. Don't allow your enemy to hold those things over your head. Take inventory on what you did before you walked with Christ and then from that point on. People will try to hold old stuff over your head from when you were in the world. You'll see that even though you may still be a "work in progress", the dirt they try to bring up since you've been walking with God, won't even come out, because the things from the past still have THEM BOUND. When you know who controls all of this, there is no need to be afraid. God will deliver on His promises. Do not allow your enemies to intimidate you because they will be cut down.

--Sennacherib continued to send threats to Hezekiah even though he himself was in a battle already. On top of that, he had someone else in line to fight him (vs. 8-9).

-A BULLY does that.

-When the threats came to Hezekiah by way of letters, he spread them out before the Lord (vs. 14-19) as part of his devotion and prayer. You'll have to read the story to see what happened to his enemy.

CONCLUSION-It is impossible for you yourself to keep your enemies from attacking you or attempting to intimidate you, but what is not impossible is for God to fight and deliver you without you having to raise a hand, knife or pistol.

## WHEN YOU KNOW THAT YOU KNOW

2 Kings chapter 18.

All throughout this chapter, Shalmaneser, King of Assyria, took Samaria and threatened Hezekiah (King of Judah) and his country to join forces with him because he was sure that the Lord WOULD NOT deliver them.

-Shalmaneser stated fact after fact as it pertained to their history and how Judah had never defeated a king of Assyria- verse 31-32 "Do not listen to Hezekiah, for he is misleading you when he says, 'The Lord will deliver us.' Has the god of any nation eve delivered his land from the hand of the king of Assyria?

***Verse 36***But the people remained silent and said nothing in reply, because the king (Hezekiah) commanded, "Do not answer him."

-*REVELATION/UNDERSTANDING*-History has played an important part in our lives. Some of us don't care about the past and then there are those who understand it's significance. The past teaches us (as it pertains to God) that God can do all things. "Will He do a particular thing is the question?"

-CONCLUSION-It doesn't matter how long it's been since God moved on your behalf, especially when you KNOW that HE still has the power to do so. Ask Him why He hasn't moved. Could it be disobedience?

## WORTHLESS

2Kings chapter 17.

This entire chapter was dedicated to replaying Israel's history of rebellion and sin, which caused them to be exiled from their land to become captives for their enemies. (Verse 7) All this took place because the Israelites had sinned against the Lord their God, who had brought them up out of Egypt from under the power of Pharaoh king of Egypt.

--VERSE 15-*********"THEY FOLLOWED WORTHLESS IDOLS AND *THEMSELVES* BECAME WORTHLESS.

*REVELATION/UNDERSTANDING*-Some of us have become so wrapped up in our "STUFF" that we've become worthless to God. We can't be used by God because we care too much about our "STUFF". We can't even hear God properly because we are to concerned with our "STUFF".

--We continue to labor for many hours because we want MORE. We sacrifice spending time with our families because we want MORE. Some of our children need our attention right now but we won't give it to them because we are working to get MORE. (And we wonder why they have gone so astray). We have accumulated ulcers and other health issues because we don't give God the quality time He should have.

QUESTION-Have you become WORTHLESS, or can God still use you?

-Whenever we decide to follow worthless idols, we can be sure that we at some point will become WORTHLESS to God.

## AMBITION VS ABILITY

2Kings chapter 14. The king of Judah (Amaziah) went forth and defeated the Edomites (verse7). Because of his victory over the Edomites, he challenged bigger and better (Jehoash, king of Israel, verse 8). Jehoash tried to tell him to celebrate his past victory and leave him and his people alone because they (Judah) were no match for him.

-Amaziah wouldn't listen which resulted in the defeat of his people and his capture.

*REVELATION/UNDERSTANDING*: Don't let your ambition lead you to be so prideful and arrogant, that you ignore sound wisdom. -Your ambition and ability alone is one thing. Your ambition and your ability with God is completely different.

## SUDDENLY

2 Kings chapters 8-10. In chapter 8, Jehu was anointed King (chapter 8 verse 6). In chapter 9 verse 6, the process took place. "(Verse 6) Jehu got up and went into the house, then the prophet poured oil on jehu's head and declared, This is what the Lord, the God of Israel says: 'I anoint you king over the Lord's people Israel. You are to destroy the house of Ahab your master, and I will avenge the blood of my servants the prophets and the blood of all the Lord's servants shed by Jezebel. The whole house of Ahab will perish. I will cut off from Ahab every last male in Israel-slave or free. I will make the house of Ahab like the house of Jeroboam son of Nebat and like the house of Baasha son of Ahijah. As for Jezebel, dogs will devour her on the plot of ground at Jezreel, and no one will bury her.'" Then he opened the door and ran. When Jehu went out to his fellow officers, one of them asked him, "is everything al right? Why did this madman come to you?" "You know the man and the sort of things he says,"
Jehu replied. (Verse 12) "That's not true!" they said, "Tell us." Jehu said, here is what he told me: 'this is what the Lord says: I anoint you king over Israel.'"
REVELATION/UNDERSTANDING: God is getting ready to do a thing SUDDENLY. One minute you will be in a particular position and SUDDENLY you will be in another. One minute your conditions will SUDDENLY change. One minute, life as you knew it will SUDDENLY be different than ever before. It will happen so fast, that people around you will not believe it.
DON'T GET IT TWISTED: It is for a specific purpose.
-Seek out the purpose

## SUDDENLY PART 2 – REVIVAL

2Kings chapter 13. There were two key verses that stuck out that I must share with you. (Verse 20) Elisha died and was buried. Now Moabite raiders used to enter the country every spring. (Verse 21) Once while some Israelites were burying a man, SUDDENLY they saw a band of raiders; so they threw the man's body into Elisha's tomb. When the body touched Elisha's bones, the man came to life and stood up on his feet.

PROPHESY: There will be a SUDDEN event that is going to happen in a short time frame, that will make those individuals who have been dead, LIVE again.

CAUSE and EFFECT-For this man, the cause of his REVIVAL, came at the hand of fact that those who were burying him SAW the group of Moabites.

(Notice the two words in verse 20-EVERY SPRING)

-Something that Historically takes place, will be the cause of a great revival.

-The Bible does not tell us who the man was, how the man died, how old the man was, or if the man even had a desire to live. One thing it does tell us is that the man was dead physically, and whether he wanted to live again or not, he didn't have a choice once he came into contact with God's anointed.

-God is going to cause something to happen that will bring the dead in contact with His Anointed.

-The dead (those who are spiritually dead, those who have given up in life, those who have become casualties to the system, those who thought that life was about a 9 to 5) won't be able to deny God's Presence and His Love. They will however, have a decision to make.

-Notice- When the man's body touched Elisha's bones, he not only came to life, but he also stood up on his feet.

--God is going to use some people to REVIVE the dead, but it is going to be up to the individual to apply some effort. He didn't lay there, but instead he got up.

-Get into position and watch- Love and light

**IS YOUR LEADER HELPING YOU?**

2Kings chapter 12 made me examine my life even closer. (Verse 2) Joash did what was right in the eyes of the Lord all the years Jehoida the priest instructed him. Is your leader HELPING you to do what is right in the eyes of God? Are you being challenged and held accountable by your leader?

--Try not to let their negative behavior influence yours.

If the not so good behavior doesn't reflect what could be "good teaching" you may want to consider finding a new leader OR exercising the -Do as I say, not as I do- principle.

**LOST**

In Ezra chapter 2, the exiles who Nebuchadnezzar had taken captive to Babylon were freed and were now returning to their homeland of Jerusalem and Judah. They were captives for 70 years and now were allowed to return home. Can you image being set free after 70 years of exile? Can you imagine being able to return to a place that your ancestors once called home after 70 years? Home was going to be a new and strange place to many and would leave many LOST. (Verse 62) "These searched for their family records, but they could not find them and were excluded from the priesthood as unclean." QUESTIONS: Have you ever felt LOST without a trace of who you are? Have you ever wondered why you do some of the things you do but have no answers? Have you ever wondered why you struggle with certain things and how you got to be the way you are: fearful, worrisome, slothful, sexual, ambitious, negative, positive, energetic, lazy, arrogant, humble etc...?

--REVELATION/UNDERSTANDING: You are who God says you are! You are fearfully and wonderfully made! Your past doesn't have to dictate your future.

--Just because they couldn't find their family records, doesn't mean they're NOT family. Just because the priesthood regarded them as being unclean, doesn't mean that they didn't still possess the gift of preaching. Just because the Governor ordered them not to eat any of the sacred food, doesn't make them less than everybody else (the governor is a man).

--YOU must ask God who you are and quit worrying about who people say you are. You must understand that you don't have the power to change what's behind you, but instead make the decision to focus on what's ahead of you. You must decide that today will be the best day of your life. You must decide that in spite of being an outcast, LOST in this world, that you will pursue God who is the only one who can answer questions that have left you LOST.

**THE PATH**

Today I want you to think about the path your on. When I was a boy growing up, my friends and I would always take this untraditional route to the grocery store. We'd walk on the sidewalk until it led us behind a long row of houses. Once you got behind the houses, the sidewalk ended and there was a bunch of weeds, trees and grass. We had to make the decision to turn around and go the long way by taking the streets, or we could make a new path by going through the weeds, tall grass and trees. We elected to take the grassy route and what we discovered was that over the years, what was once tall grass and weeds, not only became a dirt path, but the dirt path got wider and wider. Not only did we walk the path, not long after other people started riding bikes on the path and even pushing grocery carts on the path.

REVELATION/UNDERSTANDING: When you don't like the path before you, make a new one. After you make it, you'll be surprised who follows it, and the chances they are willing to try to take as a result of it.

-I can't honestly say that I was the first person to go down that grassy, weed filled landscape, but I am certain that I had a big part to play in it's expansion.

CONCLUSION: When was the last time you created a different path? The devotion this morning was inspired by Proverbs chapter 4.

## YOU EVER BEEN HUMILIATED

In Isaiah chapter 20, God used the prophet Isaiah in a way that was very humiliating. God commanded Isaiah to walk around naked for three years. He was using Isaiah to demonstrate the humiliation that Egypt and Cush would experience at the hands of Assyria (the enemy). (Verse 2) "Take off the sackcloth from your body and the sandals from your feet." And he did so, going around stripped and barefoot.
REVELATION/UNDERSTANDING: God may at times, ask us to do things that seem to be shameful and humiliating.
-I think about Magic Johnson and how he came forward with his announcement about being HIV positive. That had to be very humiliating, but it got the attention of "SO MANY."
-It can't be an easy thing to do something that will cause humiliation, but think of the "SO MANY."
-By walking around naked, Isaiah was exposed. What is God asking you to expose?

## THE SPOT

In Luke 19, Jesus was passing through Jericho when a wealthy tax collector named Zacchaeus, climbed a tree so he could get a glimpse of Jesus (because Zacchaeus was short and couldn't see over the people). A very key detail that we need to pay attention to is the fact that Zacchaeus ran ahead and climbed a tree BECAUSE he knew that Jesus was coming in that direction. My Bible says in verse 5 "When Jesus reached the SPOT, he looked up and said to him, 'Zacchaeus, come down immediately. I must stay at your house today.'"
REVELATION/UNDERSTANDING: The SPOT represents the place of connection. Jesus waited until He got close enough to

connect with Zacchaeus and then He called him out. Jesus went right where He needed to go in order to connect with Zacchaeus. He knew just how far to go.

-Some of you have loved one's who are on their way to Christ and they don't even know it. There are people who appear to have everything going for themselves but know they need to get a glimpse of Jesus for themselves. Don't be surprised when someone asks you if they can attend

a worship service with you. Don't be surprised to get a phone call from someone asking for prayer. Don't be surprised when you get approached by someone that wants to know more about Jesus.

IRONY: The irony of this connection was the fact that Jesus was the one people were trying to see but Zacchaeus was now in everybody's view.

-Jesus will call you out in the midst of people.

-Important Note: Even though Zacchaues was wealthy, he was looking for Jesus. He wanted to see Jesus for himself.

**KEEP LISTENING**

Saturday night I watched a prize fight between two high profile boxers. It was a good fight and pretty close I might add.

Nonetheless, the favorite lost the decision. They stayed around for interviews and the thing that stuck out in my mind was what this particular man that lost the fight kept saying. He kept shaking his head and repeating, "I listened to my corner".

REVELATION/UNDERSTANDING: In life we will have our share of disappointments, even those of us who are walking with God. We do things at times, expecting a certain outcome, and sometimes things don't go the way we planned it. I believe that God allows us to experience disappointment to test our character. Will we fold up and quit? Will we stop believing Him when things don't go our way? Do we only walk with Him for the things He can GIVE us (even though He's always giving us something when it seems like He's taking from us)?

-God is looking at your future and disappointment helps us to fulfill our destiny.

Conclusion: DON'T QUIT LISTENING TO YOUR CORNER, GOD REALLY DOES HAVE YOUR BACK

If you always win, nobody wants to play with you. I don't know who gave this following quote, but it seems to be so appropriate.

Love like you've never been hurt
Dance like nobody's watching
Work like you don't need the money

## WALKING INTO AN OPPORTUNITY

In Mark chapter 15 verse 21,

-A certain man from Cyrene, Simon, the father of Alexander and Rufus, was passing by on his way from the country, and they forced him to carry the cross.

REVELATION/UNDERSTANDING: Have you ever been in the right place at the right time with the right person/people- but your perception was wrong?

-Some of us have the opportunity to help someone fulfill their destiny but we are looking at it as a Burden rather than a Blessing. We often think, "I was just minding my own business" when someone suddenly drops into your life that commands your help. You may not know that you have the strength to help the individual, but you do know that the individual is struggling. Your life (as you knew it) has been interrupted and you were just minding your business.

CONCLUSION: Do you look at the situation as an opportunity to be a blessing or do you see it as a burden.

-Simon walked into a blessing. It would cost him physical labor, but he was the only one who helped Jesus carry His cross. Who are you helping to carry their cross?

## NECESSARY BETRAYAL

In Mark chapter 14 I discovered that betrayal is in many cases necessary. Betrayal is a part of the journey. Betrayal is part of purpose. Betrayal is also about discovery. Verse 17: When evening came, Jesus arrived with the Twelve. (Verse 18)

While they were reclining at the table eating, he said, "I tell you the truth, one of you will betray me- one who is eating with me." (VERSE 19) They were saddened, and one by one they said to him, "Is it I?"

REVELATION/UNDERSTANDING: We all have the potential to betray. These disciples walked with Jesus and SAW the miracles yet they still asked the question "Is it I?"

-You discover things about yourself as well as the person or people who betray you. Oftentimes we say things like "I'll NEVER do that". The truth of the matter is however; we just haven't been put into the right situations with the right people.

-Why is betrayal necessary? Betrayal gives us a clearer understanding. Betrayal brings with it one of God's principles- the NEED to forgive and be forgiven. Betrayal forces you to ask questions (God loves that). Betrayal, in many cases forces you to observe people a bit more. Most importantly, betrayal pushes us to a point where we move toward God who will never betray us.

-People on your job WILL (if they haven't already) betray you. Family members will betray you. Companions will betray you. In some cases (although not as often) parents will betray you. Betrayal only helps us to sharpen our focus on the things of God and our purpose.

-Observe how you've either been betrayed or betrayed someone else, and how it either ended a relationship, strengthened a relationship, led to a new job, led to a new real estate agent, led to a new residence, led to a better understanding.

CONCLUSION: Please keep in mind that EVERYTHING is perception. How you LOOK at situations will determine what you learn. Jesus embraced the betrayal because He understood that it was necessary to fulfill His purpose.

**PENALTY**

Over a month ago I mailed my tag renewal check and information off to the Department of Motor Vehicles and still hadn't received my sticker. Finally, I went into a DMV to get my tags renewed after waiting for over a month. I showed the people my records of when I sent it out. I showed them my bank statements of how other checks written after the check I sent them had cleared. The check hadn't been returned to me via mail and I haven't heard anything.

-I was told that I had to pay the late penalty in order to get my sticker. I was upset and ashamed of the system because I thought that I did everything that I was supposed to do, only to still be penalized.

-I paid the penalty, and went on with my day.

REVELATION/UNDERSTANDING: Even as a child of God, there will be disappointing and upsetting situations in our lives. Sometimes we feel like we follow all the rules and walk the straight and narrow line, but we still seem to get disappointed.

-Today is a new day. I got my sticker. I have my family. I have my passion. I have my health. Most importantly, I have Jesus who paid an even greater penalty.

-Yesterday is gone, forget what happened to you and look ahead to endless possibilities.

## HEARTS

Ezra chapter 1. I didn't get far in the chapter before these words hit me. (Verse 1) In the year of Cyrus king of Persia, in order to fulfill the word of the Lord spoken by Jeremiah, THE LORD MOVED THE HEART OF Cyrus king of Persia to make a proclamation throughout his realm and to put it into writing:

REVELATION/UNDERSTANDING: If God is the one who moves hearts, does it make sense to communicate to Him for change to occur rather than that anal retentive boss, that insubordinate spouse, those disobedient children, and jealous, cut-throat co-workers?

-God has given may of us promises, and like Jeremiah who was the prophet for God, God is not going to allow His Word to us to fall to the ground. He will move the hearts of the people around you in order to fulfill His word.

-Our responsibility is to believe without doubting.

-Don't be surprised when he/she comes into the workplace and makes an unexpected announcement. Don't be surprised when your children change their behavior. Don't be surprised when that spouse changes the way they treat you. Don't be surprised when an unexpected door opens so that God's promise to you will be fulfilled.

CONCLUSION: God touches hearts. Let's focus on Him rather than the individual(s).

## SADNESS PART 1

Nehemiah chapter 2. QUESTION: What is causing you Un-Happiness, Misery, SADNESS, Bitterness or Anger? Even in the body of Christ, some of us are sad because of our family life, our work conditions, our status, our culture, our community, this country and even our churches. For some of us, it is so deeply embedded in us that we can't disguise it with a smile, with a car, with a coach bag, with a man/woman, with money or promotion....

Sadness is an outward expression of what is going on inward. Sad is an adjective meaning: Grieving, Mourning, Downcast, Dull, Somber. Verse 1- I had not been sad in his presence before; so the king asked me, "Why does your face look sad when you are not ill? This can be nothing but sadness of heart." (verse 3) I was very much afraid but I said to the King, "May the king live forever! Why should my face not look sad when the city where my fathers are buried lies in ruins, and its gates have been destroyed by fire?"

REVELATION/UNDERSTANDING: There are some things in your life that are causing you this same kind of sadness to the point where it can't be hidden and must be addressed. What will you do about it??? Are you willing to risk embarrassment to lift the sadness? Are you willing to be vulnerable to lift the sadness? Are you willing to put your life on the line to lift the sadness?

CONCLUSION: Is life worth existing in, SAD, when you have the tools and passion to change things? DO SOMETHING! BE ABOUT IT!

## SADNESS PART 2: THE REQUEST

Let's revisit Nehemiah chapter 2 verses 4-6. In this particular part of the chapter, Nehemiah has made his request know to God and the king. Nehemiah found out that the king was in his corner and that he really did support him-not just with words, but with letters and finances. The Bible mentioned that when Nehemiah made his request to the king the Queen was sitting right beside him.

REVELATION/UNDERSTANDING: When it's time for you to move on and fulfill your passion, your boss, parents, teachers, co-workers who really support you should do so in their actions and not just with their words.

-I recently watched "A Raisin In The Sun" and I remember the scene where Phylicia Rashaad gave Puffy the money to start his business. Even though he blew the money and she was hurt, she loved him harder and supported him even more.

-Parents, release your kids and support them! If they make the wrong decision (ABOUT THEIR PASSION) they'll learn from it. It's not your job to KILL their dreams because you don't think it pays enough money.

-BOSSES, when it's time for someone to move on, be happy for them and do everything you can to make their journey a success. Don't be selfish and try to keep them in a place where they are not happy or where they believe their season has expired.

-Timing is everything- Nehemiah picked a time to approach the king when his wife (the Queen) was beside him. Always know when the right time is to approach a situation. The Queen in this particular equation represents the softer side. Women (not all but most) have a maternal instinct and a level of compassion that draws out the softer side of men (especially when there is no feuding).

--Above all things, after the king asked Nehemiah what he wanted, Nehemiah prayed to God first before he gave an answer (verse 4)

--Someone is on their way out of sadness. Give Him praise

**DETERMINATION: ENDING THE SADNESS**

In Nehemiah chapter 2 let's focus on verse 9-10. I went to the governors of Trans-Euphrates and gave them the king's letters. The king had also sent army officers and cavalry with me. (v.10) When Sanballat the Horonite and Tobiah the Ammonite official heard about this, they were very much disturbed that someone had come to promote the welfare of the Israelites.

REVELATION/UNDERSTANDING: Whenever you set out to free a group of people or change the negative to positive, there will ALWAYS be opposition. WHY? Because there are people who are benefiting from those who are oppressed or whose situation is negative. Then you have people who don't have an agenda of their own so they will do everything to discourage yours. Sometimes they fear that what you are attempting will make you better off than what they have or where they are.

-**When we EXPECT opposition to come, It PREPARES us rather than SURPRISES us.

--The king not only granted Nehemiah's request, but he also sent an army and cavalry to protect him.

--There's something about DETERMINATION that makes people bless you and want to help you.

How determined are you to fulfill your passion???

NOTICE: Nehemiah didn't ask the king to do the work, pay for the work or send people with him to do the work. However; he did ask the king for a little help!!!! That help was to write letters for him. Letters might be the key component missing from your strategy. Who will write a letter for you?

## CLEAR IT OUT

In Nehemiah chapter 4 let's focus on verse 10, which reads, "Meanwhile, the people of Judah said, 'The strength of the laborers is giving out, and there is so much rubble that we cannot rebuild the wall.'" Rubble is defined as broken fragments especially of a destroyed building.

REVELATION/UNDERSTANDING: many times we are trying to build something constructive in our lives but we can't because of the rubble left behind. For many of us, we try to enter into new relationships but still have rubble in our lives that won't allow us to properly build something new (hurt, hate, bitterness, credit, debt, insecurity, trust issues, controlling spirits, anger problems etc.) Don't sentence the new man/woman to the sameness that the old man/woman when you haven't given everything over to God to get over your past. Sometimes we have to be vulnerable enough to tell the new person what happened to us (not out of pity) so that they can understand what we're dealing with. This is not the time to flaunt your representative- but instead the real you. Time is too short and precious to waste on mirage.

-The first part of verse ten talks about how the strength of the laborers was giving out. It's important to note that they had already built ALL the wall to half its height.

-Have you ever started something and even though you had the momentum, something got in the way of you completing what you set out to accomplish?

-Does it make sense to swim across HALF of the Atlantic- then turn back because you're tired? Now is the time to pick it back up and finish it (catch that).

-It's amazing how we never have problems when the vision is fresh or the fruition of the vision, but instead the middle of a thing. Many times, it's not because we didn't give our best shot, but sometimes it's because God allows the weariness or temporary halting to occur so that we can seek Him for strength so that we don't believe it was under our own power that we accomplished a great thing. The people had worked hard and with all their hearts (verse 6). You can do it. It's boils down to a few simple questions.

1. WILL you do it? 2. Do you have the WILL to do it? 3. Will you expect WILL to do it for you?

## READY

In Nehemiah chapter 4, Nehemiah and his people started a project to build the wall around Jerusalem that had been mutilated and destroyed by fire. Throughout the rebuilding process, their enemies plotted against them to kill them and stop them from accomplishing their goal. Once Nehemiah found out that his enemies knew his plan, he made

adjustments that would allow his people to keep on keeping on so that their mission would be accomplished. (verse 16)
From that day on, half of my men did the work, while the other half were equipped with spears, shields, bows and armor.
REVELATION/UNDERSTANDING: There is a quote that a friend of mine used to say all the time that states, " If you STAY ready, you don't have to GET ready." Nehemiah and his people stayed ready even though unexpected events had arisen. How can you stay ready for something unexpected? Be in relationship with God, who reveals. Sometimes you may have to ADJUST, but going in to a situation KNOWING that you may have to adjust, helps you to STAY ready.
-On a more important note, if Jesus were to come back today, are you READY? Or are you in a backslidden, or non-relational place that will leave you behind?

## GO BACK

Today it is on my heart to remind you that God has already given you a seed. Philippians 1:6- He that has began a good work in you, will complete it until the coming of Jesus Christ.
-Some of us need to go back and water our seed some more (or in other words, give it nutrients). Some of us need to uproot it and plant it in different soil.
-It's not that your vision failed, it just needs to be planted somewhere else.
-It's time to go back and rediscover your seed/vision/dream.
For some of you it was singing, dancing, opening a business, going to school, or something you had/have a passion for.
-If God started it, He will finish the vision. Go Back.

## PUSHED OUT

In Genesis chapter 26, Isaac was in the land of Gerar (the land of the Philistines) with his wife Rebekah. (verse 12) In one year Isaac planted and became rich, reaping 100 fold for what

he had planted. He continued to accumulate wealth until the point where the king of the land (Abimelech) said in verse 16, "Move away from us; you have become to powerful for us."
REVELATION/UNDERSTANDING: We oftentimes NEVER leave the situation where we become wealthy (be it financial, spiritual, emotional or mental). If it's working, our natural inclination is to stay in that place because we've figured that we're doing something right or having success. But what happens when we become more powerful or just as powerful as the one in charge (be it our pastor, our boss, our principal/teacher, or a relationship)?

-Some may ask you to resign, some may ask you to step down, some may begin to conspire against you but some may have enough character and respect (as did Abimelech) to ask you to leave. WHY IT'S IMPORTANT FOR YOU TO LEAVE: it's time for you to be a leader to others. It's time for you to get OUT of somebody else's position. It's time for you to CREATE new positions for others in the next phase of your life.

-Keep in mind that God controls prosperity and wealth. What He's done in one place, he's more than able to do in another place. The anointing is not in the land. It's in the will of God.

## PUSHED OUT PART 2

The text today comes from Genesis 26: 16-23 but we will focus on verses 19-23. (Verse 17) Isaac moved away to the VALLEY of Gerar and settled there, (verse 18) Isaac re-opened the wells that had been dug in the time of his father Abraham, which the Philistines had stopped up after Abraham died, and he gave them the same names his father had given them. Verse 19- Isaac's servants dug in the valley and discovered a well of fresh water there. (20) But the herdsmen of Gerar quarreled with Isaac's herdsmen and said, "This water is ours!" (Verse 21) Then they dug another well, but they quarreled over that one also; (verse 22) He moved on from there and dug another well, and no one quarreled over it. He named it Rehoboth, saying, "Now the Lord has given us room and we WILL FLOURISH in the land."

-REVELATION/UNDERSTANDING: Isaac re-opened the wells from his father's generation BUT he didn't stop there, nor was he content on living off of what his father had done. YES it was an inheritance, but he went even further to establish his own. In other words- He added to the inheritance

-Isaac and his servants labored by digging up wells that they couldn't possess because the land belonged to someone else.

-You've got to know when to fight and when to move on.

-The key is to keep on searching because you'll eventually find what's yours.

-Never covet what belongs to someone else.

CONCLUSION: "Now the Lord has given us room and we WILL FLOURISH in the land."

-Don't think that just because you are having difficulties finding your land where you'll flourish, that it's not out there. Just don't quit.

-Isaac knew that he had a lot of resources. It was just a matter of where he would be able to settle down so he could put them to use.

-You have a lot of resources and power. You just have to keep going until God plants you in your land of milk and honey.

## RE-ROUTED

The text comes from Acts chapter 16 verse 6-10, with an emphasis on verse 7. (Verse 6) Paul and his companions traveled throughout the region of Phrygia and Galatia, having been kept by the Holy Spirit from preaching the word in the province of Asia. (Verse 7) When they came to the border of Mysia, they tried to enter Bithynia, but the Spirit of Jesus would not allow them to.

REVELATION/UNDERSTANDING: There are times when God will stop us in our tracks from going one place or doing one thing and will lead us to another place or to do another thing.

- It's important to note that, Paul's vocation/calling didn't change, only his direction.

-Has the Spirit of God stopped you from using your gifts in a particular place? Is God re-routing you? Is He calling you to move from one place to another? Is He re-routing you or ordering your steps in a different path?

-Maybe it's time to take your gifts in a different direction.

** It's important for us to know when we need to push THROUGH something to get our breakthrough and when we are being Re-routed - because when we know the difference, a few things happen

1. We don't waste time, effort and resources where we're not supposed to be. 2. We won't be as easily discouraged when doors don't open like we think they should. 3. Our perception of God will broaden because we further understand that He is leading us. 4. We can get to the people who need us the most as well as get to the people who we need. Equally important, we can get away from the people and place who don't need us and who we don't need to be around.

CONCLUSION: Paul ended up going to Macedonia to preach because He had a vision that a man BEGGED him to come there to help them. THERE ARE PEOPLE WHO NEED YOU SO QUIT BEING SELFISH, ONLY THINKING ABOUT YOUR CAREER. GO TO THE PEOPLE WHO NEED YOU. YOUR GIFTS/CALLING/PURPOSE WON'T CHANGE, YOU ARE SIMPLY PERFORMING IN ANOTHER PLACE

**IN THE FURNACE**

In Isaiah chapter 48 with focus on verse 9-11 it reads, "For my own name's sake I delay my wrath so as not to cut you off. (10) See, I have refined you, though not as silver; I have tested you in the furnace of affliction. (11) For my own sake, I do this. How can I let myself be defamed? I will not yield my glory to another.

REVELATION/UNDERSTANDING: None of us "DESERVE" God's blessings in our lives yet we often think we can conduct ourselves into receiving His goodness. He says that our righteousness is as filthy rags (Isaiah 64:6).

-We often think that if we do good, we can get saved rather than doing good because we ARE saved.

REFINED- have you ever felt like you were in the furnace; or in other words, like all hell is breaking loose in your life? Has it ever felt like no matter how faithful you try to be to God, or how close you try to walk with Him, that nothing seems to go your way? Relationships fail! The people at your job are treating you like trash – especially management! Your friends aren't there for you like you need them to be! Your money not only becomes funny, but your change becomes strange! Unexpected bills arise! The list goes on and on....

-God calls this refinement. Refinement ONLY happens in the furnace. There is a term in the jewelry business called melting and smelting. Refine by definition means- To free from impurities or waste matter. 2. Improve, Perfect. 3. to free or become free of what is coarse or uncouth.

-Perhaps you are going through some things in order to be freed. Perhaps God is teaching/showing you what you CAN live without, and quite possibly what you NEED to live without.

CONCLUSION: Precious china (dishes that sit in a china cabinet) didn't always look that good. It started out as a lump of clay and had to be 1. Pulled apart, 2. Beat. 3. Stretched 4. Shaped/molded and then put THROUGH the fire.

-You can't become precious china until you go THROUGH the fire. Don't try to get out before you are all the way done. Don't think that God is trying to kill you, because if He was, it wouldn't be that hard for Him.

-After you go through the fire, you are ready for display. You save your best china for important occasions. Could God be preparing you for something great? Could everything He is allowing you to go through be preparation to put you on display? I hope this helps.

**WE MUST TURN**

In Isaiah chapter 1, Isaiah (the prophet) is trying to get Israel to truly repent or turn away from their sins and return to the Lord. I will share a couple of verses with you starting with verse 2: Hear O Heavens! Listen, O earth! For the Lord has spoken: "I reared children and brought them up, but they have rebelled against me. The ox knows his master, the donkey knows his owners manger, but Israel does not know, my people do not understand." (Verse 5): Why should you be beaten anymore? Why do you persist in rebellion? Your whole head is injured, your whole heart afflicted. (Verse 6) From the soul of your foot to the top of your head there is no soundness- only wounds and welts and open sores, not cleansed or bandaged or soothed with oil.

REVELATION/UNDERSTANDING: This is a story geared toward Israel (God's chosen people) but how relevant is it to our own personal lives. How may times must we bump our heads doing the same things that keep us away from God? Have we taken the time to find out who God is in our own personal lives?

-In verse 6 when it talks about rebellion and being wounded, it seems like we ought to be tired of the whoopings from God. It seems like we would take a moment to look around and see what is happening to our communities. Is seems like we ought to take a moment and reflect on our current situations and spend some time thinking about how we got here.

-PERSONALLY IN OUR RELATIONSHIP WITH GOD, AND COLLECTIVELY AS AFRICAN AMERICANS

-CONCLUSION: (AFRICAN AMERICANS) Look at verse 6 "from the soul of your foot to the top of your head there is no soundness- only wounds and welts and open sores, not cleansed or bandaged or soothed with oil." Our stupidity, idolatry, wickedness, selfishness, arrogance, and division is out in the open for everybody to see. And EVERYBODY sees it but US. What must we do?
-There's only one answer and you can find it in 2 Chronicles 7:14

## NURTURED DIVIDENDS

In Ester chapter 2 (although this book is titled "Ester" and this story is about how Ester became queen) there is another individual who deserves a great deal of credit for Ester's outcome. That person was her cousin Mordecai. Mordecai took Ester in when she was just a girl and raised her because she had no mother or father. Ester also went by the name of Hadassah meaning - *nurtured.*
-*QUESTION: Who has God called* you to nurture or protect?
-Mordecai looked after Ester, protected her and gave her sound advice. Mordecai was an exile from Jerusalem meaning he came from slavery. Even though he came from slavery, he still had someone else to look after.
--REVELATION/UNDERSTANDING: You might be enslaved at your job, but you still have a responsibility to nurture someone else to make their life better. You might be enslaved in a marriage or relationship, but you have a duty to nurture someone - even though your life may be miserable. You may be in a bad place emotionally, but don't forget about the people who you are nurturing. Women-don't allow those who you are nurturing to see men running in and out of your house. And definitely don't let them spend the night. If you must fulfill those late night desires, find time to do it away from those who you are nurturing. Men - Be unselfish enough to set aside the

physical desires and take into account the kids in the house. Find some other time and place, but don't contaminate the environment where the nurtured need to be free.

CONCLUSION: Ester eventually became queen and Mordecai was more than half responsible for it. He taught her how to keep her mouth shut. He taught her how to be prudent. He taught her how to listen. He taught her how to be content. He taught her how to be ready. Ester then became queen which paid Mordecai the biggest dividend - PREPARING her to fulfill her purpose.

## WENT TO FAR

Have you ever heard the phrase "the straw that broke the camels back?" In Ester chapter 7 verse 3, the king had given Queen Ester permission to make a petition (or in other words, he asked her what she desired to have or to have happen). The queen said to the king (verse 3 of chapter 7),"If I have found favor with you, O King, and if it pleases your majesty, grant me my life- this is my petition. And spare my people-this is my request. (Verse 4) For I and my people have been sold for destruction and slaughter and annihilation. If we had merely been sold as male and female slaves, I would have kept quiet, because no such distress would justify disturbing the king."

REVELATION/UNDERSTANDING: Sometimes the enemy goes too far.

-If he would've left you as a single parent, you wouldn't of made a funk about it - but when he started messing with your kids, he crossed the line. Now you gotta pray more. Now you gotta seek God's face more. Now you can't bring just anybody up in the house.

-You wouldn't of never thought that you'd leave your "good job" but then you looked up and seen how much you've been used because it's one thing to work because you need the money and you don't have a relationship with God, but it's another thing when you realize that God is the one who supplies your needs. They had to push you; otherwise you wouldn't be starting your own company.

-He had to abuse you because you weren't gonna leave him until he did. You would've dealt with the verbal abuse and disrespectful words so it took him putting his hands on you to make you leave.

CONCLUSION: God will literally allow the enemy to push you right into HIS arms.

## HELP ME OVERCOME MY UNBELIEF

In Mark chapter 9, we read about a father whose son was possessed with a demon. Jesus showed up on the scene and the father uttered these words to him (verse 22) "It has often thrown him into fire or water to kill him. But IF you can do anything, take pity on us and help us."

-"If you can?" said Jesus, "Everything is possible for them that believe." (Verse 24) - Immediately the boy's father exclaimed, "I do believe; HELP ME OVERCOME MY UNBELIEF!"

REVELATION/UNDERSTANDING: There are times in our lives when we will come face to face with a situation or circumstance that we are powerless against. Not only are we powerless, but we give up all hope on a situation believing that there is NO way possible for the situation or circumstance to turn around. We often think that not even God can do anything with this one. As a matter of fact, we don't even take those things to God because we BELIEVE so much that it isn't

even possible, we have the attitude of "Why Even Pray About It"

-Even if we somehow gather up enough faith to know that God is able to do it, we often leave it as a thought because we don't THINK that God will do it for US PERSONALLY. We sometimes believe that God can do a thing, but we are often crippled by our own self-appointed outcome.

CONCLUSION: The father simply asked Jesus to help him with his unbelief.

-W all need to stop and ask God to help us with our unbelief. What is so big in your life and dreams that has caused you to doubt? Whatever it is, take it to God and ask Him to help you with your unbelief.

## SIN WITHIN

I'd like to start by asking a question or two. Have you ever found yourself doing something over and over again that you KNOW isn't pleasing to God? Have you ever tried to stop whatever it was you were doing, but continue(d) to relapse?

Let's take a look at Romans chapter 7.

-Sometimes in our lives, we do things or have done things NOT knowing they were wrong, until it was brought to our attention.

Example: Buying bootleg movies, getting the "hook-up" at the expense of someone else, being verbally abusive, or just not apologizing when we should. Those are just examples of some of the things we do and may not have perceived them as being wrong because everybody did it. It was the norm or socially acceptable. In Romans chapter 7, Paul talks about how he did things in his sinful nature and didn't RECOGNIZE it as sin until he came into God's law. Once he learned that what he was doing was wrong, he tried to correct his behavior but at times couldn't.

Verse 14 "For we know that the law is spiritual; but I am unspiritual, sold as a slave to sin. (15) I do not understand what I do. For what I want to do I do not do, but what I hate to do - I do. (16) And if I do what I do not want to do, I agree that the law is good (in other words you have conviction). (17) As it is, it is no longer I myself who do it, but it is sin living in me.

(18a) For I have the desire to do what is good, but cannot carry it out.

-CONCLUSION: You will NEVER get it all the way right. On your BEST day of conduct, your righteousness is but filthy rags (Isaiah 64:6) and you cannot conduct your way into the kingdom. THAT DOESN'T MEAN STOP TRYING!!!!!!!!!

-This is why YOUR relationship with God should mean EVERYTHING because God is the only one who knows YOUR HEART. Every time you apologize to Him for your sins or repent, He knows if your being sincere or not.

-The next time you find yourself doing what you don't want to do, try to remember God's mercy and grace. Your flesh WILL have a mind of it's own. It's up to us to stretch out before God and ask forgiveness. I close with a quote by an unknown person: "Grace is when God gives you what you DON'T deserve - MERCY is when God WITHHOLDS what you DO deserve."

Soak this one up and study Romans 7.

## THE FLESH

In Romans chapter 7:21 " When I want to do good, evil is right there with me. For in my inner being I delight in God's law; but I see another law at work in the members of my body, waging war against the law of my mindmaking me a prisoner of the law of sin at work within my members."

-How often have you repented for the same sin? How often have you tried to kick old ways or habits but found yourself backsliding into the same old mess? You tried praying, fasting and soaking yourself with oil - but you fell back into the same old junk.

-Paul reminds us that whatever you are struggling with and continue to fight against, most likely didn't happen over night.

-Most things we acquired an appetite for, happened over a period of time.

-Mentally and spiritually we may have the heart to do the right thing, but the flesh has a mind of it's own. The moment you acknowledge that fasting is good and that you want to push your plate back, the enemy (not necessarily a particular person) presents your favorite dish. The moment you decide to pay tithes, the bills pile up. The moment you decide you are gonna cut off some bad relationships, the phone rings off the hook with offers to treat you to somewhere.

REVELATION/UNDERSTANDING: Becoming like Christ is a DAILY PROCESS.

-It's not that you will always give in to sin, but Paul is acknowledging that the flesh has to be exercised daily in the things of God to become stronger. This is why Satan wants your mind because if he can ever get you to stop fighting or acknowledging that you need God to get into the fight with you, he has you.

CONCLUSION: Understand that the flesh and the spirit are different and that they war against each other. Although you may backslide, understand that you MUST get up and keep fighting. God looks at the heart!

-The more push-ups you do, the stronger you become. Likewise, the more you study, pray and worship God, the stronger you become. None of us can EARN our way into the Kingdom. It is purely a gift.


**EVER FELT LIKE A FOOL**

I labeled this devotion "Ever Felt Like A Fool" because I believe that at times when you follow/trust God, there are times when you feel like a fool. Have you ever felt like a fool because you trusted God for something? Maybe for someone to be healed of a sickness, maybe for a relationship to turn around, maybe for a thriving business after you left your job/security, or maybe for a loved one to return from the war.

-In any case, what happens when you yourself not only begin to trust God, but you start telling others what He is going to do for you? What happens when the person you prayed for dies? What happens when the marriage ends in divorce? What happens when your business fails? What if that person never comes home from the war?

-Today's text comes from Jeremiah chapter 20: 7-9 "O Lord, you deceived me, and I was deceived; you overpowered me and prevailed. I am ridiculed all day long; everyone mocks me. Whenever I speak, I cry out proclaiming violence and destruction. So the word of the Lord has brought me insult and reproach all day long. (9) But if I say, "I will not mention him or speak any more in His name, His word is in my heart like fire, a fire shut up in my bones. I am weary of holding it in; indeed I can not."

REVELATION/UNDERSTANDING: In order for God to even be a fire shut up inside of us, He has to have at some time revealed Himself to us in a manner which was undeniable and unmistakable.

-Nobody develops a zeal for God without a revelation of who He is.

-Jeremiah knew too much about God to stop speaking about Him. In spiteof God not doing what Jeremiah thought He would/should do, Jeremiah knew that God is truth.

-There are times in your life where you KNOW God did something for you and no matter if He never does another thing for you in life, you can't hold in His goodness. There will come a time when someone will NEED to hear YOUR testimony and in spite of how bad things might be for you at that present time, you will not be able to keep it in.

-YES it hurts at times to trust God. YES at times we feel like God has left us. YES at times we feel like God doesn't love us.

YES at times He allows us to suffer. YES at times He makes us look foolish.

-I have to take a moment to pose to you that half the time when we feel foolish, it's because we're either-trying to impress folk who don't care nothing about us, or we're trying to PROVE to him/her/them that we are spiritual/anointed.

-Remember that perception is everything. Could it be that God didn't do something to increase your faith? Could it be that God wants YOU to see if you are in it for the right reasons- or the people around you (He already knows)? Paul says in Romans chapter 3:4 "Let God be true, and every man a liar."

CONCLUSION: At the end of the day, God controls all things.

If you gotta be a fool, why not be a fool for God? Will you trust Him no matter what? I propose that you have to. No matter how bitter a blow is dealt, we all have to because you and I both know too much to go somewhere else.

"Don't Let Them Shut You Up!

## PLAY YOUR ROLE

Please pay close attention to today's

devotion because it is relevant to each and every one of us in one capacity or another. In Acts Chapter 22: 1-21, Paul, in Jerusalem at the time, had been arrested and beaten which created a platform for him to give his testimony to the Jews (which was under Roman control). Paul's testimony-verse 6: About noon as I came near Damascus, suddenly a bright

light from heaven flashed around me. (7) I fell to the ground and heard a voice say to me, "Saul! Saul! Why do you persecute me?" (8) 'Who are you, Lord?' I asked. "I am Jesus of Nazareth, whom you are persecuting,' he replied. (9) My companions saw the light, but they did not understand the voice of him who was speaking to me. (10) "What shall I do, Lord?" I asked. "'Get up and go into Damascus. There you will be told all that you have been assigned to do.' (11) My

companions led me by the hand into Damascus, because the brilliance of the light had blinded me.
(verse 9) "My companions saw the light, but they did not understand the voice of him who was speaking to me."
(verse 11) "My companions led me by the hand into Damascus, because the brilliance of the light had blinded me.
-Paul's friends were right there with him, yet he was the one God chose to be blinded by the light and to hear the voice.
-Isn't it amazing how God will allow people right in our habitat to miss something so plain and obvious? It's by CHOICE. You can't earn it. The best thing you can do is to line up with it.
-Paul's friends were there not only as witnesses, but to lead Paul to his next destination.
-Are you doing your part to help God's anointed to their destination, or are you to BUSY to see the light/anointing on them? Notice that they led Paul by the hand. There are some directions you can give with a phone call, email or text message, but then there are some directions that require personal contact. Who is God calling you closer to who physically needs you to take them by the hand and lead them to their destiny?
-It doesn't mean you'll be there forever. It doesn't necessarily mean that this is a life-long responsibility. It could only take a day. The question is, are you willing and obedient to doing your part? Hope this helps!

## *GOD STARTED IT*

I'd like to ask a question? Has hell ever broken out in your life for no apparent reason? Have things ever been turned upside down when everything seemed to be fine? Has t ever seemed like one day life couldn't be any better then the next day, life couldn't be any worse?
-Sometimes WE carry out actions ourselves that cause calamity in our lives, but then there are times when God starts

a fight? Not with you, but with Satan.

Job 2: 1-3 On another day the angels came to present themselves before the Lord, and Satan also came with them to present himself before Him. (2) And the Lord said to Satan, "Where have you come from?" Satan answered the Lord, "From roaming through the earth and going back and forth in it." (verse 3) Then the Lord said, "Have you considered my servant Job? There is no one on earth like him; he is blameless and upright, a man who fears God and shuns evil. And he still maintains his integrity, though you incited me against him to ruin him without any reason."

REVELATION/UNDERSTANDING: Many times we are the ones who cause hell in our lives. We allow people in our lives who have no business there. We frequent places where we know sin is prevalent. We allow certain influences to get us out of place when we know we should be elsewhere.

-But there are times when we are walking with God and doing everything in our power to stay faithful to Him when all of a sudden, hell will break loose. You fast, you pray, you study your Bible, you pay your tithes, you keep the commandments, you serve the homeless and hungry, you pray some more, you fast longer, you give more, you help more, you study more, you trust God more and for more - and then out of nowhere, CATASTROPHY!

-Bills come from no where, you lose your job, your family is in turmoil, your friends turn their back on you, you have nowhere to go or nobody to lean on, your spouse or significant other is trippin, your kids are out of control and you don't have any answers.

-GOD has STARTED a fight with Satan over you! Notice in verse 3 how God threw Job's name out there. Job was minding his business and all of a sudden, HELL!!!!!

CONCLUSION: If God didn't know that you would worship Him no matter what, He wouldn't allow Satan to test you. You, Me, nor Satan will ever make a fool of God.

-Maybe you're going through hell because God trusts you

enough to still give Him praise.

-Yes you might be questioning Him in your prayer life. Yes you might cry a river while you're in your prayer closet. Yes you might say some things to God that you never thought you'd say. Yes, everything might look okay on the outside, but on the inside your tore up. Yes, you are going to ask over and over again "Lord, Why Me?" I propose the question- Why not you?

-If things are that catastrophic in your life, and you've done nothing but serve God, I propose that you are one of His best.

-Look at verse 3 again, how God describes Job. If God starts a battle with Satan on your account, please know that you are one of His best and take security in the fact that NO ONE will ever make a fool of God. He will always have the last word!

## *WHOSE YEAST DO YOU PARTAKE*

Let's look at a quote Jesus said to his disciples in Mark chapter 8:15. "Be careful," Jesus warned them. "Watch out for the yeast of the Pharisees and that of Herod."

UNDERSTANDING: Yeast is often a term used by bakers or when baking bread. It is a substance used to make bread rise and only a small amount was necessary to make the whole loaf rise.

-The Pharisees were very influential people and although they were at no one time ever the majority, they could easily persuade large groups of people because they were educated, disciplined and religious people. They knew the law and were famous for putting the law above love and spirituality (which love and spirituality was Jesus' focus).

--The question isn't whether or not we have yeast in our lives, but instead, what kind of bread are we? We are all eating some type of bread and feeding someone some type of bread - be it family, friends, co-workers, students or strangers.

-Are we good bread, bad bread, half-done bread, sad bread, bitter bread, stagnant bread, jealous bread, lusty bread, hateful bread, backbiting bread, gentle bread, positive bread, negative bread, faith bread, faith-less bread? Understand?

Example: We may be kind to our children, but when we get around friends, we male or female bash because of a past relationship.

--The disciples were eating Jesus everyday but Jesus knew that even though He was the bread of life, there were people (Pharisees) who wanted to contaminate the bread He was making by way of disciples.

-You can only feed people the bread that you are made of.

-You may only be dough at this point- or need to be cooked or put in the oven of God (some people call this the furnace or fire). The fire not only cooks you to the point where you can be properly eaten, but also kills off bacteria and impurities (negativity, pride, arrogance, hate, malice etc.)

-Even though you may not be all the way cooked, your substance may be good. You just need to go in the oven a little longer.

-There will always be someone pouring or sprinkling things in our lives, we just have to be careful what we allow to penetrate us. Hope you have a great weekend. Don't eat to much bread :`)

## DOUBLE FOR YOUR TROUBLE

Today I re-visited a familiar passage of scripture by way of Job chapter 42. This is the last chapter of the book and is where God gives Job twice as much as he had in the first part of his life.

-The verse I want to really focus on is chapter 42 verse 16 which reads, "After this, Job lived a hundred and forty years; he saw his children and their children to the fourth generation."

REVELATION/UNDERSTANDING: Job went through pure hell but even though he went through, he never cursed God. Yes he questioned, yes he mourned, yes he went through tremendous grief, yes he criticized himself and at times he wanted to give up. After all of this, God gave Job an additional 140 years of life.

-How can we read information like this and worry about a

biological clock ticking, dying alone, retirement, not properly raising our kids because we are in a rush to get them out of the house to enjoy living our lives.

-We often get impatient trying to control what only God can control and that is "perfect will".

-It may cost you some tears. It may cost some heartache. It may even require some casualties. But at the end of the day, we serve a God who is able to redeem the time. At forty, Caleb was ready to possess the land God promised but the children of Israel were afraid. This caused them to wander forty years in the wilderness. God gave Caleb a promise at 40 years old.

FORTY FIVE YEARS LATER God fulfilled his promise to Caleb but the Bible says in Joshua chapter 14 verse 10-12 that, "Caleb was as strong at 85 as he was at 40." Tomorrow will take care of tomorrow - enjoy today for what today brings!

-CONCLUSION: Yesterday my wife and I went to hear a friend of ours sing at a music concert. One of the groups performed a song with a real simple verse that said, "You don't know how the day will end. You don't know if tomorrow will begin."

Hope this helps

### *CROSS IT – BUT*

In Joshua chapter 3 the writer focuses on the moments right before the children of Israel were to cross the Jordan River and enter into the *promised land.*

-The only thing that stood between them and the *promised land* was the water (or Jordan River).

-God had parted the Red Sea to let the people out of Egypt (Exodus 14) and here he parted the Jordan to let them into Caanan.

IMPORTANT NOTE: The Jordan was flood-level waters and God gave them specific instructions (the priest had to step into the waters first). We have to take the first step to getting to our promised land but how do we know what step that is without instructions?

-There are times in our lives when we have been in bondage for so long, that we are eager to get out once we see daylight. The children of Israel had to be eager to get out of bondage, even though they didn't quite know where they were going.

-There are many things and many places better than where some of us are in our lives but we may not know it because we haven't been exposed to anything but negative relationships, poverty, broken homes, corruption in the workplace, cheaters, bigots and lazy people with no ambition.

What river or obstacle is standing in your way from getting to your promised land? Can you sit still long enough to get the instructions.

EXAMPLE: When I was a kid, every summer my mother would give me, my sisters and a few of my friends theme park tickets. We were so excited leading up to the day of the event that once we finally got to the park, our first instincts (after we got the money of course) were to split up, run off and explore every inch of the park and ride every roller coaster.

-Wisely my mother wouldn't give us money or allow us to run off until she told us when and where to meet her when it was time to go home.

-You are on your way to receiving God's promises, but make sure you sit still long enough to hear God's instructions.

### SIMPLE TRUTH

Look at the verses I stumbled upon today and meditate on it. Proverbs 15: 1, "A gentle answer turns away wrath but a harsh word stirs up anger." And verse 22 "Plans fail for the lack of counsel, but with many advisors they succeed."

### IF IT WAS ME

I'd like to start by asking if you or someone you know ever said the following words, "If it was me?" Let's take a look at chapter 5 of the book of Job. This entire chapter as well as chapter 4 was spoken by Job's friend Eliphaz. Eliphaz made the mistake that many of us make, by trying to justify or give an answer as to why God has allowed us to go through such difficulty or hard times. In verse 8, Eliphaz makes the statement, "But if it were I, I would appeal to God; I would lay my cause before him."

UNDERSTANDING:

-IT AIN'T YOU! So stop saying what you would or wouldn't do in THEIR situation. We must understand that neither Job nor his friends new about the conversation between God and Satan.

--When calamity strikes, (I don't know about you) but I often try to figure out what I did wrong. I'd ask myself questions like: Was I disobedient? Did I sin against God? Was I out of place? Did I not give enough?

-We must keep in mind that there are times when we may be able to pinpoint the destruction in our lives, but also keep in mind that there is a possibility that God and Satan converse about you.

CONCLUSION: Rather than say what you would or would not do in SOMEBODY ELSE'S situation, maybe we should just pray that they will accept whatever it is God has planned for them. He ultimately controls everything anyway.

## *TRUTH TESTED*

In Job chapter 14 today, Job continues to reflect on his current situation (of losing his family, money, livestock, and business) and addresses how life can be unfair.

-It's in the unfairness of life where Job is being tested about his belief in God. In most cases, nobody thinks life is unfair when things are going well.

--Every now and again, what you "know" or "say you know or believe" about God, will be tested. "Truth untested by life's experiences may become static and stagnant. Suffering can bring a dynamic quality to life. Just as drought drives a root deeper to find water, so suffering can drive us beyond superficial acceptance of truth to dependence on God for hope and life"

-We are living in times where we are going to half to trust God or not.

-Be aware that as God continues to fulfill his Word, that there may be times when you and I are required to do something that appears to be "crazy" or "senseless".

-If you know what you say you know about God, why haven't you moved yet? Are you waiting to get fired? Are you waiting for a spouse to come to you or are you going to play offense? Are you waiting for all the money to be there, or are you going to move forward with the vision and depend on God? Are you gonna fight your vices or wait for God to take the thorn out of your flesh? Are you waiting for another hand, or are you gonna play the one you have to the best of your ability?

-We have our part to play - I promise you that God will do His part.

Closer than you think!

## *WHAT CHAPTER ARE YOU IN*

In Hebrews chapter 12 I'd like to call your attention to a few verses. verse 2- "Let us fix our eyes on Jesus, the AUTHOR and FINISHER of our faith, who for the joy set before him, endured the cross, scorning its shame, and sat down at the right hand of the throne of God."

YESTERDAY- While I was scouting locations for a movie we are gearing up to shoot this week, I ended up (long story) over at Booker T. Washington High School to watch their football team practice. My goal was to ask the coach or principal for permission to involve their school and team in our production.

Once practice was over, the coach called me over and we began to talk about how God will chasten those whom He loves and how aware He is of how to get our attention.

-After going through some very turbulent times, he said that, "I am finally to the point where I know my purpose". He went on further to say, "I've tried to leave many times to pursue offers that would've changed my lifestyle thinking that the grass was greener, only to realize that THIS is where God wants me to be."

-He is in the chapter of his life entitled "PURPOSE"

QUESTION???? What chapter are you in? Are you still trying to find out? Are you still "kickin it"? Are you in the "Isolation" chapter? (where God has set you away from everybody else). Are you in the Education/Preparation chapter? Are you in the Stiff-necked chapter refusing to answer God's call on your life (which doesn't necessarily mean in a pulpit).

WHAT CHAPTER ARE YOU IN?

CONCLUSION: Remember that Jesus is the Author and Finisher of our faith. If this is the case, then we already know the ending, but what are we doing right now in our book called life?

-The coach drew a V in the dirt on the field. At the tip of the V, he drew a line. The line represented the finish line but the two legs of the V represented two separate routes. We can either take God's route, or our route. The only problem is (and I'm sure that some of you will agree with me) that our route takes a lot longer having more turbulence, roadblocks, DANGER signs, NO TRESPASSING signs and most important DEAD END signs.

Examine your life - that will help you determine what chapter your in.

**MIGHT AS WELL**

Yesterday we wrapped up filming from our movie "When We Were Kids" and my words for you today are "You Might As Well Do It". Why???? There were actors, crew members, volunteers, people who gave donations, parents of the talent, and most importantly kids - who were inspired to go out and live their dreams after being on the set. Not solely because of me, but because of everybody coming together to make one man's vision come to pass. The environment was positive and energetic. Even though we were delayed because of rain and behind on schedule, NOBODY expressed any anger or frustration.

--CONSIDER what God has planted inside of you. YOU MUST GO AFTER YOUR DREAMS When you refuse to go after YOUR dreams, you STUNT the dreams of the people destined to be in your path.

-SOLOMON says in Ecclesiastes chapter 2 (and I quote 10-11) " I denied myself nothing my eyes desired; I refused my heart no pleasure. My heart took delight in all my work, and this was the reward of all my labor. Yet when I surveyed all that my hands had done and what I had toiled to achieve, everything was meaningless, a chasing after the wind; nothing was gained under the sun."

REVELATION/UNDERSTANDING: Even though Solomon was talking about living for God and being righteous, I want you to focus on the part about him laboring.

QUESTION? WHY ARE YOU KILLING YOURSELF IN A PLACE WHERE YOU ARE MISERABLE? DO WHAT GIVES YOU JOY AND BE WILLING TO DOWNGRADE YOUR LIFESTYLE IF NECESSARY TO BE JOYFUL.

## *IS IT WORTH IT*

In Judges chapter 1 verse 12-13 it reads, "And Caleb said, 'He that smiteth Kirjath-sepher, and taketh it, to him will I give Achsah my daughter to wife. (13) And Othniel the son of Kenaz, Caleb's younger brother, took it: and he gave him Achsah his daughter to wife." Is It Worth It?

-Othniel was willing to put his life on the line for the daughter of the king. This meant that he would become a member of the family and have access to whatever the daughter had as it related to the kingdom.

-His money problems were over, his land problems were over, and he could ask anything of the king that either he or his daughter wanted.

REVELATION/UNDERSTANDING: Not only were the instructions to SMITE, but also to TAKE. In other words, if you do something for the king, the king will do something for you.

-If you do something for God, God will do something for you.

Caleb could've taken the battle himself, but he gave someone else the opportunity to be elevated.

-CONSIDER your circumstances- God can GIVE you material, wealth, a significant other and anything that your heart desires, but are you willing to risk something to get it? Are you willing to put your life on the line to go to the next level? (Not literally your life, but your lifestyle).

-Keep in mind that fulfilling part of the instructions isn't good enough. You must go all the way! Is it worth it????? Is the reward worth the sacrifice? Is the elevation worth the risk?? Is the outcome worth the process?

-What is God asking you to do to go to the next level?

## *EVER WONDERED?*

Have you ever wondered or thought about what THIS life is all about?

-Some of us spent our early days being educated or prepared to get a "job". Some of us have strived to accomplish the unthinkable and impossible. Some of us have and continue to live our lives in pursuit of money and material gain. Some of us have lived in pursuit of a man/woman to make us happy or to fill the void of us being alone.

-Some of us do everything we can to become health nuts in an effort to live longer rather than live healthier (as if we will never die). I pose these scenarios and ask the question again

- What is this life all about? Money can only buy so much. You can only have but so much sex. The role of a car is to get you from one place to the next so why do we "need" so many at one time?

-I believe we often thrive for people to look at us. We desire to be seen and feel significant. We desire compliments. We desire to be acknowledged. We desire credit.

-Although these things come with humanity, What is THIS life all about? I pose these questions for one reason and one reason only. We all have an end in THIS life. Could our purpose be to fulfill the assignment(s) God has set before us?

-CONCLUSION- ECCLESIASTES 12 verse 13- Now all has been heard; here is the conclusion of the matter: Fear God and keep his commandments, for this is the whole duty of man."

## *GOD KNOWS YOU'RE SCARED*

In Judges chapter 7 we find the story of Gideon and how God would use him and 300 men to fight against and defeat thousands of men. It's important to note that Gideon started off with 32,000 men and after God screened them, he only had 300. Lets focus for a moment on verses 9-10. (verse 9) During that night the Lord said to Gideon, "Get up, go down to against the camp, because I am going to give it into your hands. (verse 10) If you are afraid to attack, go down to the camp with your servant Purah and listen to what they are saying. Afterward, you will be encouraged to attack the camp."

REVELATION/UNDERSTANDING: God knows when we are afraid to take a step toward something He's inspired us to do. He knows that as people, we tend to look at the giant in front of us rather than the God whose behind us.

Since He knows this about us, there are times when He will drop nuggets of inspiration or send us signs or confirmation about moving forward.

-Our duty is to remain open and willing to move in obedience.

-A step toward marriage can be fearful but for someone today, this is the right decision. If your gonna live married, you should be married. You are already performing the tasks that it takes to run your own business, but you have always depended on a paycheck so you are fearful to live without the crutch or "security" of one. GOD KNOWS IT! But He equipped you to step out on Faith and you CAN'T pay attention to the recession.

-The sooner you accept and admit that you are afraid, the sooner god will send you confirmation that He has your back. The question is- Will you move once He says move?

-God had already prepared a sign for Gideon to give him the confidence he needed to do what God had called him to do.

-CONCLUSION- Just because you may be fearful, you are not excused or exempt from doing what God is calling you to do. All I'm saying is that, God knows when your scared.

-Rather than beat around the bush, Ask God to give you confirmation that will increase your courage and faith to go forward with your assignment.

## *THE DASH*
Good day! I studied Judges chapter 10 and discovered something within the first 5 verses. Tola and Jair were two people who judged Israel for a total of 45 years, YET the only thing we read about them is that Tola lived in the hill country of Ephraim and that Jair had 30 sons who rode on 30 donkeys and controlled 30 towns. THAT'S IT. Then you don't hear anything else about them.
-REVELATION/UNDERSTANDING: When we attend grave sights or read obituaries, You see the person's name and then it has the date of which they were born THE DASH and the date they died. THE DASH represents what we've done with our lives.
-There is a lot of information represented within that DASH but is it worth noting? 45 years of Israel's history from the standpoint of leadership could be summarized in 5 verses.
-Do you live the type of life that isn't worth noting? When your life is over, what will people remember about you or say about you? What attributes and stories would you like your children to tell about you or be told about you? What kind of chances have you taken? What kind of risks have you taken? How many people have you helped? How has your character developed by giving up something that was/is no good for
you or the people you love? What habits have you broken?
CONCLUSION: Is life worth living faithless or pursued without greatness & conquering your territory? What would your DASH say about you? Are the things your doing now or within your life WORTH NOTING?

## *PLANTED FOR A PURPOSE*
Genesis chapter 1 verse 8 'Now the Lord God had planted a garden in the east, in Eden; and there he put the man he had formed.'

REVELATION/UNDERSTANDING: God creates situations for our lives so that we will work His plan/creation.

-In the verses that follow, you'll see that God also put everything in the environment that was needed for the purpose to be fulfilled. Not only that, what could and could not be done in the environment was stated (RULES).

-Consider your environment and your purpose. You have been planted there for a reason. Do you understand why you are there?

-It's important to note that it was God that put you there so don't get so high-minded and think it was your doing. It was God who put you there!

-What are you doing with it?

## *MIS-INTERPRETED SACRIFICE*

Last night I got a phone call from one of my closest friends and he had a question/statement that pertained to selfishness. Without going into to many details, he talked about relationships in his life and how people depend on him so much- to the point that if he decided that he was going to take a month off to get away and take some time for himself, the other party would NOT be in agreement. It's important to note that he is not married nor does he have any children.

-He feels like he sacrifices and gives a lot to his community and family and in spite of giving of himself, when he mentions taking some time for himself- it is totally unacceptable.

REVELATION/UNDERSTANDING: It doesn't matter how much you GIVE to the other party if they don't tap into or fully recognize what you do as GIVING. The same goes for LOVE - SACRIFICE - TRUST - and any other attributes we possess within our character.

CONCLUSION- We often don't properly interpret what a person does and what they consider to be significant if WE don't see it as THEY see it. You can give a person all of your cell phone passwords, pin numbers, email address passwords etc. all in an effort to get them to trust you, but if THEY don't see it as you opening yourself up and giving them access to your personal business - then they CAN'T fully appreciate what you've done. Maybe trust for them means that you stay in the house and have no social life. Maybe it means that you have separate bank accounts. Maybe it means that if you don't talk about your weaknesses, then you haven't been honest and therefore aren't worthy of trust.

BOTTOM LINE is that you must be understood in order for there to be one accord. Take time to understand how the other party feels about what it is THEY are doing so that you can properly interpret it's significance in your relationship.

## WHEN THE FORCE IS AGAINST YOU

In Acts chapter 27 Paul (accompanied by other prisoners and centurions) was headed to Rome by boat to be tried before Caesar. On their journey, a strong wind came against them and made it difficult for them to reach their destination.

(Verse 7) - We made slow headway for many days and had difficulty arriving off Cnidus. When the wind did not allow us to hold our course, we sailed under Crete, opposite Salmone. (Verse 8) We moved along the coast with difficulty and came to a place called Fair Havens, near the town of Lasea. (Verse 9) Much time had been lost, and sailing had already become dangerous because by now it was after the fast

REVELATION/UNDERSTANDING: This quote "May The Force Be With You" was a phrase used in the movie Star Wars to wish people luck, generally when an individual parted ways or the object was facing some sort of imminent challenge. The phrase implied the speaker's wish that the power of the Force would be working alongside the addressee, in order that the addressee's goals would be more effectively accomplished. But what happens when the force is against you???

-This particular force during Paul's journey was the wind.

-There are times in our lives where although we have our eyes set on a destination and a time to arrive there, circumstances beyond our control rise up that could DELAY our arrival.

-It doesn't mean that we won't get there, but there is a possibility that we could be delayed, re-routed, or both.

No matter how well we plan our lives!

-The Bible says in verse 7 that they made slow headway and then it says that the wind did not allow them to hold their course.

-It might seem that the little headway you are making is a drop in a bucket when your vision or destination is gigantic.

-Take the little victories! Don't despise them - embrace them!

-And when your strength is depleted and you've done all that you can, pull over and take your hands off the wheel and coast. It doesn't mean you've given up, it means that you fought for so long until your muscles need a rest. Don't think that you've failed because God allows circumstances in your life that will make you coast from time to time.  Maybe God wants you to spend some time coasting because during this time you will build a relationship with some unbelievers.

-Perhaps you've had so much success sailing through life, that you never took the time to see or be amongst those who are stuck, shipwrecked or overboard.

CONCLUSION: (verse 8) We moved along the coast with great difficulty and came to a place called Fair Havens.

- Even though you are coasting (not pedaling, rowing, driving or doing anything that requires your physical strength), it is difficult to sit still in this type of situation because we are still so eager to get to our destination.

-Don't worry - this too is a part of the journey called LIFE. LIFE is a journey- not a DESTINATION Enjoy the view as you coast, because there will be a time to use your muscles again.

May The Force Be whatever it's supposed to be for You this season!

## *BLOCKED FOR YOUR PROTECTION*

In Genesis chapter 1-3 I studied the story of Eve and Adam a bit. I discovered through this text that God will block things from you, to protect you.  In chapter 3 verse 6, EVE TOOK fruit from the tree of life that God told her not to and GAVE some to Adam to eat- and he ate it.

IMPORTANT: Eve GAVE to Adam and he ate it.

Verse 22- And the Lord God said, "The man has now become like one of us, knowing good and evil. He must not be allowed to REACH OUT HIS HAND ALSO and take from the tree of life and eat, and live forever." (23) So the Lord God banished him from the Garden of Eden to work the ground from which he had been taken. (24) After he drove the man out, he placed on the east side of the Garden of Eden cherubim and a flaming sword flashing back and forth to GUARD the way to the tree of life.

REVELATION/UNDERSTANDIG: It's one thing to be FED something by someone else, but something completely different when YOU yourself REACH OUT YOUR HAND to partake of it yourself.

-Don't you start introducing or exposing people to wrong-doing.
-The punishment isn't as severe when you are seduced into sin as opposed to being the one seducing. Yes there are consequences on both sides but they are much more severe when you are the perpetrator.
-God had to block some of YOUR desires because they would've destroyed you. God has blocked some people that you would normally be head over heals for because they would've turned you out. There were some people who have STD's who you would've given yourself to, but God blocked your emotions from getting involved. God blocked some business deals that would've made you lose your religion and soul later on down the road. God blocked a job that you wanted (not because you weren't qualified, but because He didn't want the people there to be blessed by your presence. Nor did He want you in some situations for the next 30 years because had He allowed you to get the job- you would've never left to pursue your Passion and Purpose with the intensity you would've needed to attain it. You would've been burned out with no energy left.

-God will make whatever it is so hard to get to, that you'd be a fool to even make an attempt at it.

NOTICE how God put a Cherubim (or mighty angel) at the entrance as well as a flaming sword that moved back and forth to guard the way.

-Monitor the blocks in your life and switch your perception to why it could be blocked for your protection.

### *EVICTED*

In Genesis chapter 3 God showed me something else in verse 23: So the Lord God banished him from the Garden of Eden to work the ground from which he had been taken. (verse 24) After He DROVE the man out, he placed on the east side of the Garden of Eden cherubims. The word DROVE is the Hebrew word Garash meaning: to drive out from a possession; to expatriate or divorce.

REVELATION/UNDERSTANDING: Has God ever had to drive you away from somewhere? Has God ever had to divorce you from some nouns?

-Our problem is the fact that we don't want to be divorced from the thing(s) that will ultimately kill us - and sometimes we know that it WILL kill us.

Expatriate: is a person living in a country and culture other than that of the person's upbringing or legal residence.

-You can't stay where you are because God has other plans for you.

-Adam got evicted to be saved - not destroyed. Yes eviction might be embarrassing! Yes eviction might be inconvenient! Yes eviction can put you on the street or in an unfamiliar place! Yes eviction might be the end of a chapter in your life; however, in order for there to be the beginning of something, there has to be an ending to something.

-Who is God evicting from your life? What is God evicting from your life? Where is God evicting YOU from?

-Try to be in a place where you embrace the eviction of God. Be it your job, relationship, family or residence. God is only setting you up for something greater.

# THE BEGINNING!

Go!

CONTACT

J. White
President/CEO
**FISHERS OF MEN PRODUCTIONS LLC**
Office: (213) 840-1001
info@tapintoyourdestiny.com
www.tapintoyourdestiny.com
www.fishersofmenproductions.com
www.destinybrandsllc.com

## DEVOTIONAL SERIES

# COME CHANGE SEASONS PURGE GO

## BY J. WHITE

## DEVOTIONAL SERIES

# Exude
## Walk With
# COURAGE
### Be Strong & Of Good
### Not For The Faint Of Heart

## BY J. WHITE

# DEVOTIONAL SERIES

## Practicing Your Walking in FAITH Necessary Living By Increasing Your

### BY J. WHITE

# DEVOTIONAL SERIES

# KNOWING YOUR SELF-WORTH
## UNCOMPROMISING YOUR
## BELIEVING YOUR

### BY J. WHITE

## DEVOTIONAL SERIES

# WALKING IN
# LIVING ON
# PURPOSE
# UNDERSTANDING
# LIVING WITH

### BY J. WHITE

## DEVOTIONAL SERIES

# Understanding Your Purging Embracing RELATIONSHIPS Purpose in Releasing Building Healthy

## BY J. WHITE

# DEVOTIONAL SERIES

## Having peace in the
## Integrity in the
# WORKPLACE
## Keep your soul in the
## Seasons in the

### BY J. WHITE

There is a saying that goes that all men are created equal but does the same go for women? Insanity has been defined as doing the same thing over and over again and expecting a different result. But the dictionary states that insanity is the senselessness and foolhardiness of a person who is usually not in their right state of mind.

The Sisterhood of Insanity is based on the lives of ten women who all have a story to tell. Come ride on a roller coaster of mystery and emotion with ten intriguing yet familiar women. These are real women that we know, see and love everyday but what is so amazing is that what we see is not usually what we get.

$12.99
ISBN 978-0-615-41624-3
51299>
9 780615 416243

*URBAN LIGHT*
*is a poet and author*
*who writes inspirational stories*
*about life's hardest lessons*

# Sex is a good thing...

## & the **Church** ought to embrace it —

## & **Preach** about it,

---

*...but we women aren't holding our breaths.*

### Let the conversations begin...

- Sex in Singleness
- The Gospel of Good Sex
- Unmasking Sexual & Spiritual Truths
- Q&A—Tough Questions, Real Answers
- Reclaiming Goodness as Sexual & Spiritual Beings

REGISTER TODAY at *sexNspirit.wordpress.com* for *webinars & workshops* that create safe space & sincerely speak to women's sexuality in the context of faith.

- No topic is off limits!
- All adult women (18+) are welcome.
- Anonymous/pseudonymous participation is available.

---

Your host, *Dr. Candi Dugas,* is in her 16th year of ministry, celebrating life with a love for G~d and G~d's people that promotes faith, freedom, and justice. A member of Decatur United Church of Christ, she believes our faith traditions may be thousands of years old, but our thinking doesn't have to be. She lives in Midtown West Atlanta with her beautiful daughter, Jordan. *For more about Candi and her work* — *candidugas.com*.

# OVERWHELMED?
## ...Can't do it alone?

### We're here to help you reach your goal.

Providing Life Coaching and Business Consulting for Individuals, Small Businesses and Non-profit organizations.

www.extreme-overflow-enterprises.com

## Extreme Overflow Enterprise, Inc
Cultivating inspiration for divine destination.

Made in the USA
Charleston, SC
18 August 2012